Fanny Johnson

A thoroughly modern Victorian headmistress

Bolton High School for Girls
1888-1893

Veronica Millington

Published by Royd House
The Book Case
29 Market Street
Hebden Bridge
West Yorks.
HX7 6EU
www.bookcase.co.uk

Cover illustration: Sixth Form Group, Whitsuntide 1892

We apologise in advance for any unintentional
omissions or errors, which we will be happy to correct in
future editions.

ISBN: 978-0-9556204-8-5

Foreword

In 1984, I became librarian at Bolton School Girls' Division where I inherited a beautiful hand-crafted cabinet, donated by Miss Higginson, an earlier Headmistress. It contained "The Archives".

Here, I came across an insignificant-looking exercise book—Fanny Johnson's logbook detailing letters and visits she received from parents as Headmistress between 1888 and 1893 together with her responses. The contents were riveting. I realised I was reading a piece of unique social history—unseen by anyone outside the school. It was striking how much had changed: the coal fires, the cook with diphtheria, the children dying of infectious diseases, the pupil who was one of only two surviving children out of a family of ten. Yet so much was familiar: the petty squabbles between pupils, complaints of too much homework, parents taking children on holidays during the school term—not to mention the odd flashes of exasperation and wry humour from the Headmistress. There must, I thought, be many people—not just those connected to the school—who would be as fascinated as myself to discover and learn about the minutiae of daily life in a Victorian school. My ambition was to see it in print, available to the public.

The time seemed to have arrived when Veronica Millington retired from teaching English at the school in 2006. Veronica, already an author and for many years the editor of the school magazine and newsletter, had intended using her "leisure" time to pursue an interest in researching her family tree. So, by 2007, when she had had a year of retirement in which to hone her detective skills, she seemed to be the ideal person to write this book.

Veronica agreed and that was the beginning. We were fortunate that we had a complete picture of the school at that time. As well as Fanny Johnson's logbook we had the School Council [Governors'] minutes, all the accounts, Inspection reports, the schemes of work, Form Mistresses' comments on the pupils in their class, the first school magazine and, last but not least, a full set of one girl's reports for that period. We could not have had a better foundation.

What we knew about Fanny Eliza herself, however, would have fitted onto the proverbial postage stamp. Who was she? Where had she come from? What sort of person was she? Was she a trailblazing Headmistress? How would she be viewed by society? Veronica tackled all these questions and, despite the difficulty of retrieving ordinary women's stories in that period, she found the answers.

A picture began to form, not only of Bolton School and its particular history, but also of a wider society, where girls' education was a new notion and women were fighting for their rights in all spheres of life.

What Veronica discovered at the heart of all this was a free-thinking, radical, liberal, warm-hearted, thoroughly modern Headmistress: Fanny Eliza Johnson 1888–1893.

Linda Frew
Senior Librarian
Bolton School Girls' Division, 2008

Contents

Illustrations

The log pages referred to in the following list are taken from Miss Johnson's thirty-seven-page logbook which records the letters and visits she received from parents during her five years as Headmistress.

1888	
Date	Subject
Feb. 6th	Cold caught at school
Jan. 27th	Too much home-work
Feb. 16th	Arith. not been explained
Mar. 12th	Mother calls that she is grieved about torn book, & offers to re-place it. Gert: is delicate & excitable only two left out of ten.
Mar. 8th	Mother calls — that Ada is deaf — She is grieved about book & has seen a boy on the Tues: morns looking over a hedge.
Ap. 10th	Mother calls — that she is very ill & obstinate & is to leave off home-work —
Ap. 10th	Mrs B. calls that she is grieved & surprised at their bad report —

February-April 1888.

Chapter 1

From foundation
to fourth headmistress

1877 was an interesting year. Thomas Edison invented
the phonograph, the explorer Henry Morton Stanley
came to the end of his epic 7,000-mile journey down the
River Congo from its source to the sea and finger-
printing was used for the first time by Hirschel of the
Indian Civil Service. Annie Besant and Charles
Bradlaugh's book on birth control led to their conviction
for obscenity and Giovanni Schiaparelli observed
"canals" on Mars. On the political front, Russia declared
war on Turkey and Queen Victoria was proclaimed
Empress of India by Prime Minister Benjamin Disraeli. In
the Arts, 1877 saw the publication of Tolstoy's *Anna
Karenina* and the first performance of Tchaikowsky's
Swan Lake while, on the sporting front, the first-ever Test
Match took place between England and Australia.
Australia won, of course!

Anyone scanning the pages of the Bolton newspapers at
that time for rather more local news, might have come
across the following item on June 20th: "A High Class
School for Girls will be opened at the Mechanics'
Institution in September next. The Course of Instruction
will comprise a sound English Education, with French
and Latin Languages. Further particulars in future
announcements." So ran the first public announcement
of the formation of the school which would, over
subsequent decades, evolve into Bolton School Girls'
Division.

The whole process had begun a mere five weeks earlier at a meeting, held on May 14th, of the General Committee of the Bolton Mechanics' Institution at which it was decided that a joint committee should be established for the purpose of setting up a day school for girls. The group, which was clearly forward-thinking, had also stipulated that the committee should include "six ladies representing various shades of opinion". It is perhaps not surprising that a significant number of this committee were nonconformists, Bolton having long held the reputation of being the "Geneva" of the north on account of its strong Puritan views.

Notable among the prime movers of the scheme were Mr and Mrs William Haslam, who were prominent members of Bank Street Unitarian Chapel. Their interests had always lain in the fields of public service and, in particular, education, as was the case with many other prominent Bolton nonconformists. One such was J P Thomasson, who became the first Chairman of the School Management Committee. A member of the Free Christian Church and later of Bank Street Chapel, he was a great benefactor to the town and would become Liberal MP for Bolton in 1890. One of his most significant contributions to this new enterprise was to ensure financial stability for the school in its first two "trial" years which he did by setting up a Guarantee Fund—a shrewd move prompted by the recognition that demand for this kind of education was by no means certain. [Interestingly it would appear that he also helped Manchester High School for Girls—which had opened just three years earlier—by lending them £10,000 at a very low rate of interest, thus enabling the work on their new building to be completed.]

Mrs Mary Haslam 1851-1922.
Founder and Governor.

Mary Haslam was a suffragist, a prominent member of Bank Street
Unitarian Chapel and the first woman Poor Law Guardian in Bolton.
Her daughter, Winifred, said that the High School was "almost all my
mother's idea".

Another notable member of the Bank Street congregation was Mr Isaac Barrow, the son of committed Unitarians. He was to maintain a high level of involvement with the new school, acting as Secretary to the governing body until his death in 1890. As well as being the superintendent of the Bank Street Sunday School, he had served as Secretary to the Mechanics' Institute before becoming its president in 1874. A forward-looking man in educational matters, he was an early advocate of technical colleges.

In realising their dream of setting up a day school for girls, the school's founders were placing themselves among the front-runners in an educational revolution which was beginning to sweep the country. A mere thirteen years earlier the Taunton Commission had reported on "the wretched state of girls' education". Middle class girls were largely taught by governesses who provided a "social" education designed to fit their charges for polite drawing rooms. This usually involved little more than deportment, music, drawing and French. More serious study would have been seen as not only "irrelevant" for girls but also potentially disadvantageous—any hint of the "bluestocking" being a possible handicap in the marriage stakes. The few schools that catered for lower middle class girls were poorly staffed and of a very low standard indeed.

In an attempt to address this woeful state of affairs, the Commission recommended that "schools run on the lines of the North London Collegiate should be founded on the outskirts of every town". Originally begun as a family venture in 1850, North London Collegiate was by then in the redoubtable hands of Frances Buss, the daughter of its founding family. She had confidently outfaced the widespread doubts about the aptitude of girls and young women for learning—not to mention the alarmist notions about the physical damage they might inflict on "themselves and their reproductive systems through over-exertion at their lessons".

Borne along on the wave of enthusiasm generated by the recommendations of the Taunton Commission, groups of dedicated campaigners for women's education began to found high schools up and down the country during the final decades of the century. Particularly in the north, these often built on the work of the Mechanics' Institutions which had for a good number of decades been providing a combination of self-help, educational and social groupings for adults. As early as 1854, the Leeds Mechanics' Institution had set up a ladies' branch offering "a practical education which included, as well as the basic subjects, classes in accounts and book-keeping" and access to its school of art, laboratories and libraries.

Bolton nonconformists had always been enthusiastic supporters of this movement, founding Bolton Mechanics' Institute in 1825 and this, combined with their centuries-long involvement with the Boys' Grammar School and the later Bolton High School for Boys, makes it scarcely surprising that by May 1877 they too were taking the first steps towards setting up a girls' day school.

No school can function, of course, without a Head Teacher and so in mid-June an advertisement appeared for "an efficient Lady Teacher to conduct the proposed

Bolton Day School for Girls to commence early in September". As well as organising the school the successful candidate would be required to teach Reading, Writing, Arithmetic, Grammar, Geography, English, History and Needlework. Almost as an afterthought it was decided that French and Latin "would also be preferred". While the proposed salary of £100 was extremely generous for a woman in that period, much was expected of her, especially as the salary was only guaranteed if "the whole of the subjects named can be taught".

By early July things were moving on apace. Applications for the position of Lady Principal had been received from five ladies—three married, two single. Interestingly, the three married ladies had their letters and testimonials returned immediately—whether as a result of a lingering prejudice against married women working outside the home or because of poor qualifications we shall never know. Whatever the reason, the appointment of a Lady Principal was adjourned pending the re-advertising of the post.

By mid-July, with eleven applications received and scrutinised, it was agreed that a Miss Kean and a Miss Seymour should be shortlisted. On the day of the interviews the committee read three further applications, each of which was deemed "not worth consideration", before taking the unanimous decision to offer the post to Miss Eliza Kean. With this significant appointment made, all that remained was to recruit the first cohort of pupils and so on August 3rd, with the prospectus finally approved and despatched to the printers, it was agreed to place advertisements for pupils in the "Evening News", "Chronicle" and the "Manchester Guardian".

At the end of September, with only three days to go, Miss Kean submitted a list of textbooks to grace the new cupboard which had been purchased just a fortnight earlier. Then, as a final act, the management committee visited the School Room. We can get some idea of the basic level of equipment that greeted those first pupils when we learn that this inspection led to the decision to provide a cupboard for slippers as well as a larger one for books and work and a platform for the teacher's desk and seat. With these last purchases made, everything seemed to be ready for the new educational venture. From the initial proposal back in May, to the opening of the school doors to pupils on October 1st 1877, the whole process had taken a mere twenty weeks.

On that first morning just twenty-two pupils crossed the threshold of the Mechanics' Institute in Mawdsley Street to begin their school careers. Their accommodation consisted of one room and, in addition to the subjects specified above, they would also be studying French and Latin. Needlework, as we have seen, was included—a concession no doubt to those practical domestic skills that young ladies were supposed to have. Notably absent from the list, however, was any form of sport. "Drill"—a strange mixture of wand and dumbbell exercises and marching—would be introduced at a later date, as would a form of cricket known as "Stumps".

Teething troubles were inevitable, of course. Ominously, in view of later financial problems, a number of parents had still not paid their fees two weeks into the term—the cost then being four guineas a year for girls over the age of ten. More importantly, it was already becoming clear that, because of the "varied attainments" of the pupils, there was too much work for one member of staff and so an assistant teacher was advertised for. The matter of cleanliness was also raising its head, judging by the fact that the Hall Keeper was to be allowed 3/- a week for additional cleaning: the school rooms and staircases were to be "swept and dusted each day and the floors scoured not less than once a fortnight".

On the positive side, the curriculum was already broadening. A number of visiting teachers and lecturers were engaged—which must have caused quite a stir as all of them were male, except for the dancing teacher and Mlle Barr, one of the French teachers. November also saw the school acquiring a new name, Bolton High School for Girls, its third in six months. The committee agreed to the purchase of a small desk bell and a map easel and to the probationary engagement of a young assistant mistress from Halliwell—sadly, her appointment was terminated after only three weeks. More or less the last decision taken in that first term was that "arrangements must be made for the more efficient heating of the school".

Having begun in such a forward-looking manner the foundation was determined to remain at the forefront of educational developments. At the school's second prize giving in 1879 the speaker, Professor Wilkins, condemned the fact that able girls were being refused admission to the new day schools because their parents were "in the retail trade". Clearly an enlightened man, he urged that all day schools should be absolutely free from snobbery and class distinctions. His remarks did not fall on deaf ears and not long afterwards a system of free scholarships was set up. The school was also seeking to recruit two more assistant teachers and it was suggested that, as well as using the normal channels, enquiries should be made of "Miss Buss and other friends" about suitable candidates for the posts.

In those early years Headmistresses did not seem to stay for long. When Miss Kean left in 1880, the school advertised in a London paper for a "first class Headmistress". The successful applicant—twenty-nine-year-old Quaker, Mrs Sarah Corbett—was certainly quite a catch. As Sarah Woodhead she had been one of the first students at Girton and one of the first three to sit the Mathematical Tripos[1] in 1873. She had even been immortalised in the College song which urged all its students to "give three cheers for Woodhead, Cooke and Lumsden, the Girton pioneers!" After successfully completing her Mathematical Tripos examinations she had moved back to her native Manchester where she became one of the first teachers at Manchester High School for Girls in 1874. A few years later she had married architect and surveyor Christopher Corbett and, with two small children to care for, was running her own school on Silverwell Street in Bolton.

---

[1] Opened in Hitchin in 1869 and transferred to Cambridge in 1873, Girton was one of the first colleges for women—closely followed by Newnham. Both colleges would later become full members of the University of Cambridge. "Tripos" refers to the final honours degree examinations at Cambridge University.

When she was appointed as successor to Miss Kean in 1880, the sensible decision was taken to amalgamate the two establishments and to move to larger premises on Chorley New Road—an area which was to become the school's natural home, remaining so to this day. Times continued to be difficult, however. The school was still struggling to attract sufficient pupils and, by the end of her second year, Mrs Corbett's health had deteriorated to such an extent that she was left with little option but to resign.[2] To add to the school's difficulties, Mrs Thomasson, a prominent member of the governing body, had sent a letter in the November of 1881 saying that she and her husband "advised the discontinuance of the School unless there was a promise of thirty pupils". This obviously prompted a serious discussion as to the advisability of carrying on, especially as there were "only eighteen certain promises for next Term".

Fortunately, courage prevailed and Mr Haslam proposed that the school should continue and that half the financial guarantees should be called in before December 31st. In an attempt to boost pupil numbers he also suggested that a circular should be sent to the "parents of promised pupils", saying that the school was continuing and urging them to use their influence to help the management committee. The circular also mentioned that a Junior or Preparatory School would be set up for pupils under the age of ten, at a fee of two guineas per term.

---

[2] Mrs Corbett eventually went on to become an examiner for private schools. In 1904 she edited "Extracts from the Vahan" for the Theosophical Publishing Society—the last mentioned work arising out of the resurgence of interest in reincarnation.

On December 28th 1881, following the resignation of Mrs Corbett, thirty-year-old Miss Vokins accepted the post of Headmistress. Strikingly beautiful and youthful-looking, Kate Vokins had completed her university course four years earlier—one of the first students of Newnham and only their second ever to pass the Tripos examinations in Mathematics—and had then gone on to teach Mathematics at Nottingham Girls' High School in 1877.

With financial matters on a slightly more even keel, Bolton High School for Girls now began to make steady progress under her leadership. It also had yet another change of premises, this time moving further up Chorley New Road to "Hopefield". Then in October 1887, after six years at the helm, Miss Vokins resigned, having been offered the Headship of Blackburne House School in Liverpool—the sister school of the Liverpool Institute for Boys.

With only a matter of weeks remaining before Miss Vokins' departure at Christmas, Mr Haslam was asked to write to the University Society for Women Teachers "with the view of obtaining a suitable successor and, in the event of this failing, an advertisement was to be inserted in the 'Atheneum'. Salary to be £200 per annum, with a capitation allowance of £1 per annum for each pupil in excess of fifty". The doubling of the salary paid in 1877 possibly reflects how much more onerous the job had become.

At a Special Meeting on November 9th, Mr Haslam reported back to the committee on the interviews which had just been held with a Miss Sheldon and a Miss Bate. He then read out a letter from a third applicant, Miss

Fanny Eliza Johnson, who for personal reasons was unable to attend the second round of interviews. She had, however, already been interviewed a week earlier and had at that point been considered "most suitable". This letter seems to have more than confirmed that favourable impression and the committee quickly agreed that an immediate offer should be made to Miss Johnson—who by an interesting coincidence had been an assistant teacher at Nottingham High School at exactly the same time as Kate Vokins. By early December Miss Johnson had accepted the position along with a salary that was almost certainly well in excess of what she had been accustomed to. She had also been given her first task—to "secure a replacement" for a long-standing member of staff who was leaving to study for a degree.

But who exactly was this woman whose interview and letter had so impressed the selection panel? Obviously her background, character and values must have struck a powerful chord with those who were about to entrust her with the task of educating the girlhood of Bolton—and it goes without saying that these same factors would inevitably play an important role in how she chose to run the school.

So, before joining Fanny Eliza Johnson on her first day as Headmistress, we need to turn the clock back some ninety-four years and head off to Huntingdonshire in order to find out exactly who she was.

Dec. 4th — Mother calls (having given notice) & says she has been suffering all the term — with headache & backache &c — aged 15 — Change one just begun —

Nov. ? — Mother calls to say she has seen Dr Roth — & is to take gymnastic excercises': She is not straight. It's "these desks & high schools" — change not begun —

Dec. 18th — Writes to "protest" agst subscription to platform for entertainment — Waddington père also refuses to allow Theresa to pay !

1889.
Jan. 22. — Mother calls that she worries so abt lessons — is not well & is to stay at home for term — Mother calls — Lily to leave at Easter (for India) & to do as little as possible 3 guineas' worth — M. is not to sing — because of her throat —

December 1888-January 1889.

Chapter 2

The Johnsons of Llandaff House

If, in the light of the role she was about to take on, Fanny Eliza Johnson had been able to choose the family in which to be born, she could scarcely have done better than the Johnsons of Llandaff House.

The patriarch of the family was Fanny Eliza's grandfather, William. He was born in 1793 in Ramsey, Huntingdonshire, the son of a baker. Gifted with a sharp mind and a great desire to improve himself, young William had quickly come to the attention of a local clergyman who offered to teach him Latin. He evidently took to his studies for, so the story goes, he used to carry a Latin Grammar around with him in his wicker basket, learning sections of it as he delivered bread for his father.

William's first opportunity to taste life beyond Ramsey came in 1809 when, at the age of sixteen, he was offered work as a groom in Cambridge. As things turned out, however, that particular job came to a remarkably swift end when Mr Pennington, realising that his new employee knew next to nothing about horses but was well versed in Latin, promptly engaged him as a tutor to his son instead. And so, from this humble beginning, William Johnson's career in education took off. By the time he was eighteen he had secured a post as assistant teacher in a private nonconformist school in Cambridge run by a Mr Newton Bosworth. Then, at the age of twenty-one, he returned to Ramsey where he set up a school of his own and, two years later, married Eliza Barker, a local teacher.

A view looking north along Regent Street c 1920.
Llandaff House with its portico entrance is in the left foreground.

Back in Cambridge, meanwhile, Newton Bosworth's nonconformist academy for boys had moved to Llandaff House on Regent Street. However, the work of running the school eventually proved too burdensome for him and in 1823 he announced that his former assistant, William Johnson, was to acquire the school and take over as Headmaster. Under Johnson, who was already by then a noted Classicist, the school began to thrive with its mix of day pupils and boarders, the basic cost of board and tuition being thirty guineas. An advertisement of the time offered any potential scholar not only every requisite to help him prepare for university but also "every domestic arrangement calculated to promote his comfort". Chief among the domestic comforts must have been the school dinners—the sight of enormous joints being turned on a spit before a great open fire would be a familiar feature of the house for many decades to come.

A view of Llandaff House
showing its portico entrance and the adjoining property
shortly before demolition in 1932.

For the next eighty years, the commodious Llandaff House would also be the Johnson family home and it was there that Fanny Eliza's grandparents raised and educated their four children. The house was ideal for the growing family. The garden at the back not only led into the semi-private grounds of Downing College—an open space about a third of a mile long with fields and trees—but also gave onto the much-loved "Grove" to which only the Johnsons and their next door neighbours had access. Better still, the rambling old house, parts of which dated back to the seventeenth century, had numerous passages, trapdoors, big lofts and secret spaces, all of which "gave an air of mystery and romance to the house, especially in the eyes of the children".

William Henry Farthing Johnson, Fanny Eliza's father, was born there in 1825, the third of four children. They were all very able: Eliza, the eldest, eventually became joint Head of a Preparatory Boys' School in Birmingham while Henry Isaac, the youngest, became Headmaster of the Royal Institution School in Liverpool after a period in South Africa and at Cheltenham College. Tragically, William's elder brother James died when he was only nineteen, having just gained a place at Christ's College, Cambridge.[3]

William himself studied at Corpus Christi but was unable to graduate fully because, as a member of the Baptist church, he was not prepared to make the obligatory statement of affiliation to the Church of England. In fact he would have to wait a further twelve years to be granted his BA, one of the first two Cambridge nonconformists to be allowed to do so after the University Act of 1857 opened most degrees to dissenters. In the interim, however, he gained a BA from the University of London which had been founded on a non-sectarian basis partly in order to help those whose professional lives were suffering as a result of the religious restrictions at Oxford and Cambridge.

Having returned to Llandaff House as a teacher of languages, William Johnson took over from his father as Headmaster in 1851. Typically, he threw himself wholeheartedly into the education of his pupils—and into their games and pastimes, often playing cricket with them on Parker's Piece, a large stretch of open land opposite the school. He was above all a man with a

---

[3] Unless otherwise stated, all colleges subsequently referred to are those of the University of Cambridge.

strong social conscience: he served as a JP and found time to involve himself in the welfare of Cambridge young people in general, becoming the first President of the Cambridge YMCA, which he had helped to found and where he was actively involved in educational work, and later of the Sunday School Union as well. He also served as deacon at the Baptist Chapel for forty-five years.

As for William Johnson senior, although he had retired to Ramsey soon after his son became Headmaster, he continued to visit the family home until his death in 1871. Years later, his youngest granddaughter Alice recalled him as a "somewhat remote figure—a personage to be treated with great respect—for whom were reserved the best place by the fire and the plate of hot buttered toast. He sat there in state, sometimes playing chess, more often smoking his long clay pipe." Apparently his grandchildren would watch eagerly for the moment when the long stems of his pipes inevitably broke, for then they could be used for blowing the best soap bubbles imaginable.

Fanny Eliza's mother was Harriet Brimley, second daughter of the impressively named Augustine Gutteridge Brimley. Originally from a family of Bedfordshire farmers, he had risen to become a prosperous Cambridge grocer and alderman and, by 1853, had been elected Mayor. A religious man, he had been made a deacon of St Andrew's Street Baptist Church in Cambridge in 1823—a position he would hold for many years.

Augustine Brimley married, in succession, Hannah and Harriet, two of the nine daughters of James Gotobed[4] who was the proprietor of the Bull Hotel. However, it seems to have been James' second daughter, Anne, who was the leading spirit of both the Gotobed and Brimley families. A strong character with a good sense of humour, she was virtually self-taught and a voracious reader. It eventually fell to her to bring up the four Brimley children—George, Caroline, Harriet and Fanny—not only in the period between her brother-in-law's two marriages but also following the early death of his second wife in 1833, possibly in childbirth. Anne's influence was profound: she instilled into the children her own great love of books and an unswerving commitment to service.

It was Augustine's second daughter, Harriet, who married William Johnson in 1851 and it is no surprise to discover that her love of literature, and of Tennyson and Wordsworth in particular, became a feature of their early life together. Harriet named her eldest daughter after Wordsworth's "Lucy" and, despite the need for stringent economies, William always made sure that she had the latest volume of Tennyson as soon as it was published. Nor is it any surprise to find her throwing herself with characteristic zeal and commitment into the role of Headmaster's wife, acting as matron at Llandaff House and teaching regularly in the school. However, her health was far from strong and this, combined with the pressures of bringing up her growing family on very

---

[4] Augustine's first wife, Hannah, died in 1825 at the age of thirty-five, having given birth to Caroline not long before. It was Augustine's subsequent marriage to Harriet which resulted in the birth of Fanny Eliza's mother in 1830.

limited means, forced her to give up—although she still taught German and Latin to the occasional pupil.

Harriet's two sisters also allied themselves to families whose lives revolved around books and scholarship. In the spring of 1851 Caroline had married their brother George's closest friend, Alexander Macmillan. He and his older brother Daniel had been Cambridge booksellers since 1845 and co-founded the Macmillan publishing company at around the same time. They published the works of many eminent contemporary writers, a number of whom became regular family visitors. Among these were Thackeray, Charles Kingsley and Tennyson, the last being fondly remembered for his reading of "Maud" in the Macmillan drawing-room. Sadly, Daniel—whose posthumous claim to fame is that he was the grandfather of Prime Minister Harold Macmillan—died prematurely in 1857. This was the same year in which George Brimley died, also tragically young, depriving Trinity College of its librarian and the literary world of a highly valued critic.

In 1863 Alexander Macmillan moved to London to manage his growing publishing business. As a consequence, Robert Bowes, one of the firm's London employees and also a Scot, was transferred to Cambridge to run the family bookshop which duly changed its name to "Macmillan and Bowes". Five years later Robert married Fanny, the youngest of the Brimley sisters, and moved to Park Terrace with her—a matter of yards from Llandaff House. Despite the Macmillans living in London, strong links were maintained between all three families, strengthened no doubt by business interests and a shared love of literature and new ideas.

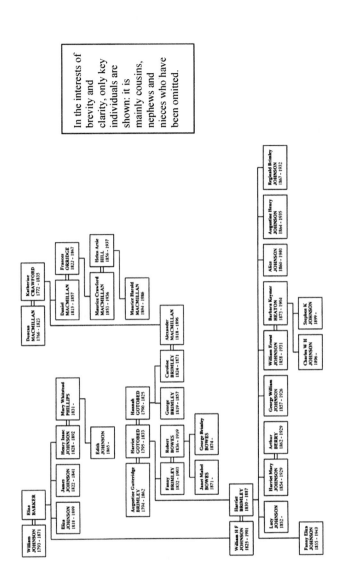

In the interests of brevity and clarity, only key individuals are shown: it is mainly cousins, nephews and nieces who have been omitted.

A perfect illustration of their closeness was a happy occasion in the summer of 1877 when the Bowes, Macmillans and Johnsons all went on a summer holiday together to the Isle of Arran, the original home of the Macmillans and a place they all loved for its natural beauty.

Such, then, was the family into which Fanny Eliza had been born on November 30th 1855, the third of William and Harriet's eight children. By the time she was five, the family home in Regent Street was shared with Elizabeth Thornton, the Governess, as well as eighteen boy boarders aged between nine and sixteen, an unspecified number of day pupils, two assistant masters, one cook, one housemaid and two nursemaids. Despite running a very successful school which was supported by many leading Cambridge academics, William and Harriet clearly felt it preferable, at least in the case of their younger children, to send them elsewhere to complete their education. George and William, for example, would eventually attend the Perse School in Cambridge, with William then moving on to his Uncle Henry's school in Liverpool, while their youngest sister, Alice, would spend the four years between 1874 and 1878 at Miss Haddon's School in Dover.

Fanny and her older sister Harriet do not appear to have been sent away, however. By the time they were fifteen and sixteen respectively, when we might have expected to find them at boarding school, they were both still at home—at least according to the census of 1871. The entry describes them as "Scholars and Teachers" and, while it is not possible to say for certain, it seems fairly likely that Llandaff House was not only their home and school but also their place of work. At that point the academy was still maintaining its numbers yet the lives of Fanny and her siblings were constantly overshadowed by their parents' anxieties as they struggled not only to make ends meet for their family but also to keep the academy going in the face of increasing competition from the endowed schools which were gradually crushing private schools out of existence.

Nonetheless, these must have been exciting times for Fanny. Not only was she living at the heart of one of the foremost academic cities of Europe but she was also growing up in a family whose lives revolved around learning and books. Years later it was said of her younger brother William Ernest—who by then was a lecturer at King's College—that he would frequently sit by the fire at Llandaff House, swathed in a red shawl and engrossed in animated conversation with his undergraduate students. One can imagine that things were not so different when Fanny was a fifteen-year-old, no doubt constantly overhearing lively discussions between her parents and their older "parlour boarders"—not to mention the academics and Cambridge notables who seem to have been frequent visitors.

Given the climate of the times, the burning question of female emancipation would surely have been one of the most frequently debated topics at Llandaff House and one which was guaranteed to be given wholehearted support by the Johnson family. In the wider world campaigns were getting under way to address not only the issue of women's political rights but also their right to a decent education. In 1867 Anne Jemima Clough, who would eventually become the first principal of Newnham College, had formed the North of England Council for promoting the Higher Education of Women—a move which resulted in the development of lectures and university-based examinations for aspiring women teachers. In January 1870 a similar scheme of lectures for women was set up in Cambridge by various members of the university, chief of whom was Henry Sidgwick.

To Fanny and her sisters 1871 would have seemed like a veritable "annus mirabilis" for it was then that a hall of residence was set up, only a matter of yards from their home, for women who wished to stay in Cambridge in order to attend such lectures. The hostel, which initially housed just five students, was supervised by none other than Anne Jemima Clough and it was out of this establishment that Newnham College grew, its numbers boosted in 1880 as a result of the merger with Henry Sidgwick's own association for the promotion of higher education for women.

As women's colleges were still disapproved of by many members of the university it was felt advisable for those early students to remain as unobtrusive as possible. Certain restrictions were therefore imposed on them such as not riding bicycles in the main street, not taking a boat out on the river after nine in the morning—unless accompanied by a College don or a married woman—and not being seen in the town without gloves and hats. Other restrictions, while more predictable, were surprisingly rigid—not only were female students banned from entertaining men in their rooms but they were not even allowed to invite female friends in to meet their fathers and brothers. The presence of a mother in the room apparently made no difference whatsoever to the ruling! Yet, despite these irritations, the simple fact of being a pioneering student at Newnham or Girton must have felt hugely liberating and exciting.

Not surprisingly, their progress was avidly followed by the Johnsons, particularly as all four daughters would soon spread their wings in the world of education and scholarship. As far as Fanny's eldest sister, Lucy, is concerned, there is little more than census information to go on but it would appear that after initially working as a governess in London she found employment at a school in Cromer. But her career would be seriously curtailed when, in her forties, her eyesight deteriorated very markedly. Indeed, all the Johnsons were extremely short-sighted with George and Alice also on the verge of blindness in their later years.

Fanny's elder sister, Harriet, became a fully-fledged assistant teacher and continued to live and work at Llandaff House. Then, on March 21st 1877, Fanny herself was appointed to Nottingham High School for Girls at a salary of £100 a year. Although there was no general requirement in this period for teachers to have official qualifications, the Girls' Public Day School Trust, of which Nottingham High was a member, preferred to appoint qualified staff where possible. So, while Fanny Eliza appears not to have taken a degree course at either Newnham or Girton[5], she almost certainly had appropriate qualifications for teaching—possibly taking

---

[5] While it has always been assumed that Fanny Eliza was a graduate of Newnham, their archives contain no record of her ever having been there. Nor do those of Girton.

the Cambridge Higher Local Examinations, a route favoured by many aspiring women teachers at that time. She remained at Nottingham for four years before moving on to Croydon School in March 1881. Five years later she left and returned to Cambridge, possibly because of the increasingly fragile state of her mother's health.

Finally, thanks to the good fortune of being born just at the "right" moment, her youngest sister Alice was able to go up to the newly-founded Newnham College in 1878—the first step on what was to be a distinguished career. Blessed with an "acute and critical mind" she gained a First Class in the Natural Sciences Tripos in 1881. This was the first year in which women had the right to sit the Tripos examinations officially and have their results formally recognised—previously they had depended on sympathetic examiners and invigilators making special arrangements for them to sit the examinations informally. In the year following her Tripos, Alice was awarded a Bathurst studentship[6] and then went on to study for her MA. For six years from 1884 she worked in the college's new Balfour Laboratory as Demonstrator in Animal Morphology before becoming Private Secretary to Mrs Henry Sidgwick, the college Principal, in 1890.

Many years later Alice would be described in her obituary as daunting, stern, rigorous and eagle-eyed. Yet the writer also took great pains to note that, beneath her dry and exacting manner, there was a woman of strong human sympathies who had great integrity and a highly-developed sense of justice—as well as a delightful

---

[6] An award of £50 a year made to Natural Science students.

34

sense of humour. It appears that all these characteristics were typical of the Johnson family as a whole.

Of course, it was still by and large a man's world, and one in which greater opportunities and honours were open to Fanny's brothers—most notably George William and William Ernest. After graduating from Trinity as Eighth Wrangler[7] in 1880, George entered the Colonial Office where he would rise to the position of Principal in 1900 and, in 1905, be awarded the Companion of St Michael and St George for services to British interests abroad. A man with a profound sense of justice, he spent most of his time at the Colonial Office trying to stamp out the shameful exploitation of prostitution, opium smoking and gambling in the Eastern Colonies.

Despite being prone to debilitating asthma attacks all his life, George's younger brother William Ernest was to have the most academically distinguished career. By the time Fanny Eliza had been appointed as Headmistress to Bolton High School for Girls, his list of academic honours was already impressive: having been admitted to King's in 1878 as an Exhibitioner[8] he had graduated as Eleventh Wrangler in 1882, going on to gain 1st Class in the Moral Science Tripos in 1883 and an MA in 1885. He would become a Fellow of King's seven years later and play a leading part in the development and teaching of moral science in the university. An inspirational teacher and good conversationalist, he also fitted the popular

---

[7] "Wrangler" is the term used for those placed in the First Class of the Mathematics Tripos: Senior Wrangler, Second Wrangler and so on.
[8] "Exhibitioner" denotes a student who has been awarded a scholarship.

stereotype of the brilliant but absent-minded academic, constantly losing umbrellas, train tickets, pocket books and purses—much to his family's affectionate exasperation!

Given the nonconformist tendency to treat men and women equally it is no surprise to find all the Johnson men avidly supporting the growing clamour for female emancipation and for women's equal access to education—with George possibly foremost in this. He was a keen supporter both of the suffragists[9] and of the campaign to allow women to have their degrees conferred on them. Alice recalled that he never failed to go up to Cambridge to register his vote on their side whenever any proposal on women's degrees was brought before the Senate. It was to be a long struggle which brought many setbacks and sharp reminders of the deep hostility with which the idea was viewed, such as the occasion on May 21st 1897 when the latest defeat—by 1713 votes to 662—was greeted in the town with jubilation, bonfires and fireworks. Thankfully, however, George did live to see the day in 1921 when Cambridge University was finally empowered to confer "Titles of Degrees" on women.

So now we can rejoin Fanny Eliza in the final days of December 1887, shortly before her departure for Bolton. Regrettably, her mother Harriet had died a few weeks earlier at St Andrew's Psychiatric Hospital in Northampton, following a mental breakdown. Indeed it was the gravity of her condition that had prevented

---

[9] Campaigners for women's voting rights whose tactics were less militant than those of the suffragettes. Millicent Fawcett, of whom more later, was a key figure in this group.

Fanny from attending the second round of interviews at the High School which had taken place on November 9th, the day before her mother died.

William Johnson, however, was still very much a force to be reckoned with in the world of education when, in January 1888 and at the age of thirty-two, his third daughter was preparing to take up the reins as Headmistress of Bolton High School for Girls, the fourth person to fill that role in the school's eleven year history.

1889.

Jan 22. Mother calls – long talk – that G. is not much attached to her teachers – is not well – likes popularity & those that like her – loves acting –

Jan. 31st Mother complains windows open in class-room (five minutes on acct of smoke) & so child has caught cold – The scarlet fever has left her throat weak.

" 29 I call to explain that reports were sent – tho' they have not arrived

" 14th Furious correspondence abt my well-meant advice –

Ap. 29th Mother calls to give notice – & that H. is very unhappy because she thinks she is not a "favourite" ∴ E. Tillotson was scolded more than she for writing notes during examination –

Ap. 30th Mother writes that she is dis-appointed about report –

January-April 1889.

Chapter 3

A new phase of existence

The school that Fanny Eliza Johnson took over at the start of 1888 comprised fifty-four girls and three assistant teachers, including twenty-three-year-old Fannie S Jarvis who had arrived just a few months earlier. Two members of staff from Miss Vokins' era—Miss Ledward who had left to do a degree and a temporary teacher, Miss Richardson—had been replaced by Miss Jackson and Miss Berry. Clara Berry was in fact not only Miss Johnson's first appointment but also a family friend, their brothers both being noted mathematicians at King's. As well as the school's full time members of staff there were also four "visiting teachers" for piano, drawing, Latin and French.

To take on the mantle of Headmistress in an unfamiliar school and with a staff that was almost entirely new to the establishment must have been extremely daunting. But Miss Jarvis, who to all intents and purposes provided the sole link with the previous term, proved her worth and, in Miss Johnson's words, it was as a result of her "cordial co-operation that the labours of the new comers were very much lightened."

As regards the curriculum, there was apparently a widespread feeling amongst fledgling girls' high schools that it did not do to offer fewer subjects than boys' schools—or indeed different ones—as this would be seen as a virtual admission that girls were less able than their male counterparts. Certainly, the curriculum that Miss

Miss Johnson, Headmistress 1888–1893.
The picture forms part of a permanent display of
Headmistresses' portraits
at Bolton School Girls' Division.

Johnson inherited in her first term was broadly in line with that of most comparable schools: Scripture, Literature, Grammar, History, Geography, French, German, Latin, Arithmetic, Mathematics and Physics as well as Drawing and Music.

Not all forms studied exactly the same subjects, however. In Form I, for instance, the only language studied was French and, strangely, there was no English Literature at all—at least according to their Spring Term scheme of work. By the time girls reached Form III Literature was included—ranging from "A Midsummer Night's Dream" to Tyndale and Spenser—as were Physical Geography and Latin. But it was not until Form V that German, Physics and Mathematics proper, including Algebra and Euclid, were being taught— Euclid being the 3BC Greek mathematician whose great work "Elements" was the standard Geometry text up to the end of the nineteenth century if not beyond that.

By the Summer Term Miss Johnson had already made a number of adjustments. Form V had gained Trigonometry at the expense of Physics while the top stream of Form III had made a start on Algebra. Given Miss Johnson's love of all things literary, the unaccountable lack of literature in the lower forms had been speedily remedied by the introduction of Poetry and Reading. Had the pupils seen the titles of the poems they were to study, however, they might have had mixed feelings for, nestling cheek by jowl with "Scenes from Fairyland", Tennyson's "Sweet and Low" and "The Coming of Spring", were "Dead Bird's Song" and "Child's First Grief". And they had only just recovered from a term studying the small matter of "the Earth etc, the World and Europe". At least they only had to deal with England in the Summer Term!

The school had just emerged from an Inspection which had been carried out the previous September by a Mr Pincher, BA. Having made many very favourable comments, particularly regarding the teaching of Mathematics, History, Literature and Geography in the higher forms—venturing so far as to say that "the attainments of some of the pupils are of unusual excellence"—he had been fairly scathing about two aspects of the work in particular. As regards the teaching of French he had noted that the girls' pronunciation was "distinctly bad" and that "some alteration seems desirable in the teaching of this subject". Mr Pincher's main concern, however, was in relation to the lower forms. In his opinion the teaching was "too mechanical" with too much "mental drilling and learning by rote" while insufficient efforts had been made "to awaken the intelligence of the pupils by object lessons and other methods of sense teaching".

Such a comment might have struck a real chord with Miss Johnson whose grandfather William, in an address to the friends and supporters of Llandaff House Academy nearly sixty years earlier, had railed against the kind of teaching in which "much information had been given but little knowledge acquired." We shall never know whether it was Miss Vokins or Miss Johnson who first addressed this issue but certainly by the Spring Term of 1888 Form I were already getting stuck into their Object lessons on "bees, physiological botany, ponds and ditches" under the guidance of Fannie Jarvis. By the summer they were having fun working their way through an eclectic list which included cocoa, tea, coffee, coral, flax, the ear, the senses, whalebone, salt and pepper!

Of course no school operates in a vacuum and parental input was as important then as now. Luckily, we have the Headmistress's thirty-seven-page log to give us a flavour of the contacts between home and school, whether in person or by letter. Occasionally Miss Johnson also entered a brief indication of her response. Compared with the copious entries for later years Miss Johnson's log for her first two terms is relatively short. Possibly this was a brief "honeymoon period" when parents were quietly gauging their new Headmistress before bombarding her, as they certainly would do later on, with numerous letters and visits.

Beginning on February 6th the log is dominated by some very predictable topics—health, overwork and behaviour—and by April Miss Johnson had received the first of many letters that were to arrive during her time as Headmistress expressing distress and surprise at a "bad report". Judging by parental reactions over the next five years we get the impression that report comments were rather more forthright in those days. Obviously we do not have access to the reports themselves—except in one particular case—but what we do have are the various form mistresses' brief remarks about each girl in their class. If these provided the basis for the formal reports that were sent home, then quite a few parents must have been left wondering why anyone was prepared to teach their reprobate daughters at all!

According to the character sketches penned beside their names the girls were rough, lazy, impolite, self-satisfied, untrustworthy, sulky, conceited, flighty, peevish, tiresome, ungracious and disrespectful—with "fidgety" and "noisy" being the most prevalent of their lamentable traits! A number of pupils were labelled as cowards, rule breakers, mumblers and dawdlers, while the more specific comments included "dirty books", "appears to copy", "harm to desk", "babyish about Euclid", "cruel to companion", "writing a disgrace to school" and "headaches from eating sweets"!

It has to be said, however, that positive remarks such as "a pupil we value", "kind, helpful", "dear polite little girl" and "very satisfactory work" far outweighed the negative ones and, as noted before, there is nothing to indicate that the most scathing of the "in-house" remarks were sent home in *exactly* the same form as they appeared in the class lists. It is rather to be hoped not!

Apart from leaping to the defence of their wayward daughters, parents were also keen to inform the school of anything that might be creating difficulties for their child. One mother called in about her daughter's deafness while another wanted to explain that her child was "delicate and excitable"—the kind of comment that would become a considerable irritation to Miss Johnson in a few years' time. On this occasion, however, the mother would have received nothing but sympathy for she went on to reveal that her daughter was one of only two surviving children out of ten. No wonder she was anxious to protect her: life must have seemed so much more precarious in those days.

We also sense some slightly ambiguous attitudes to schooling. One parent wrote in to excuse her daughter's absence because of a cold which, she acidly pointed out, had been "caught at school" while others objected to "too much homework" and to "too much written work" being set. As it was only a few years since serious fears had been expressed about the physical damage that over-exertion at school might inflict on girls such concerns are scarcely surprising. And then there was the mother who worried about the comparisons, helpful or otherwise, that might be made between sisters once they went to school. "Mrs A calls that Lucy may do ball exercise, she is not strong or so clever as Elsie, worries over lessons, has too much. She would like them both to do the same work."

The most interesting entries for these first two terms, however, relate to an incident which involved two girls—Gertrude and Ada—and a torn book. Mortified about the damage, Gertrude's mother called in offering to replace the book, Ada's mother having already visited the school to say that she was very "grieved" about it all. That should have been the end of the matter but within a month Gertrude's mother had returned to say that her daughter was "very ill and obstinate and was to leave off homework" followed a few weeks later by a letter announcing that she would be leaving at the end of term. As Gertrude was none other than the "delicate and excitable child" whose mother had lost eight children, Miss Johnson immediately paid the family a visit. Once there she quickly established that the cause of Gertrude's distress was her unshakeable belief that her teachers did not like her "since the affair of the torn book". Happily, after plenty of reassurance no doubt, Gertrude was persuaded to stay on.

There was also the occasional bizarre communication in the logbook such as the one recorded on March 8th: "Mother calls that ... she has seen a boy on the Tuesday mornings looking over a hedge." He was clearly conducting a school "inspection" of a very different kind—perhaps a sign that girls' schools were still something of a novelty! If only Miss Johnson had made a note of her reply.

Another aspect of Miss Johnson's role was, naturally, to work alongside the governing body, or the School Council as it was known. Looking at the minutes of the meetings for those first two terms it seems that money was as tight as ever and even the smallest of purchases had to be approved. The first such requests from Miss Johnson were for a wall map of France and, three months later, for two nine-foot forms for the Assembly Rooms. Matters of pupil numbers and fees inevitably loomed large, particularly as the financial situation was still far from secure. However, it is clear that Miss Johnson was prepared to go to some lengths to retain certain pupils even when their families could not afford any increase in fees. This at least would seem to be the obvious inference to be drawn from the entry dated May 9th: "The following suggestions by the Headmistress were agreed to: namely that Maggie and Lillie be allowed to remain at the Three Guineas Fees, on condition of assisting as Student Teachers."

Doubtless this solution to Maggie and Lillie's problem also helped to address yet another difficulty noted in the

Inspection report of the previous September—that "three permanent members of staff, including the Headmistress, are insufficient for the five forms—especially as they had been further subdivided in several subjects". Mr Pincher's depressing conclusion was that "much better results will not be achieved while this situation continues". With the recruitment of one extra member of staff at the start of the Spring Term and, now, two extra Student Teachers, things were probably a little easier.

These same minutes also reveal that Miss Johnson was more than capable of adopting quite an individual approach to the curriculum. Prompted by the desire to embrace female emancipation and to prove that girls could cope with exactly the same curriculum as boys, many girls' schools had probably gone a little too far in avoiding traditional domestic subjects. However, in doing so, they could be—and indeed had been—accused of ignoring a very real need of girls, most of whom were destined to be wives and mothers anyway. So it is interesting to see the following entry in the minutes for July 4th: "Miss Johnson, having a prospect of securing some Cooking lessons for some of the older pupils during next term, it was resolved that the use of the school kitchen shall be lent for the same and for similar classes." This surely suggests some independence of thought from a pragmatic and practical woman who was guided by sound common sense.

While it is certainly true that many girls up and down the country were very excited to be following the same academic curriculum as their brothers, this unexpected opportunity to develop "domestic skills" was recalled with real pleasure and appreciation by Fanny Smethurst, a pupil of the school from 1888-1896. "We had formal lessons only in the morning, the afternoons being given up to preparation, with special classes in art, needlework and crafts. This last subject was, I am sure, not at all usual at that time and we loved it, being allowed to choose whether we would paint, make mosaic teapot stands or writing boards etc. Later, a select few of us were invited to go, one evening a week, to the house in Ducie Avenue where the three mistresses lived and learn to make baskets. We also had an annual exhibition of work, combined with competitions in cookery, recitation and pencil sharpening." A ringing endorsement indeed, even if the last item seems somewhat bewildering!

As the Summer Term progressed and thoughts started to turn inevitably towards more seasonal pursuits, Miss Johnson and the governors decided to combine the annual Sports Day with a Garden Party. Promised an allowance of £5 towards the expenses, Miss Johnson was given the go-ahead to make all the necessary arrangements for the event. With light refreshments provided as well as entertainment from a String Band, it all sounds rather appealing and a fittingly happy ending to her second term as Headmistress.

1890.	Subject.
Sep. 17.	Father calls - She has weak heart -
"	I write to ask if she can take Camb. Exam'n. Father comes.
"	To leave off music without notice -
"	Leave without notice - Notice - because of our reports being unfavorable!
"	Mother writes that she will try to get over pulka
"	Mother objects to my providing dinners!
Oct. 15.	She has gone home feeling sick, probably J. being "purring round" in play-time. Notice
Oct. 17th	Her father calls - She is "doing lessons" till 9.30 -
Oct. 24th	Mother writes she has a bad cold + sore throat prob: increased by going out in the thin shoes in the garden at play time
Oct. 23rd	As only just begun "change" M. also - Both not estab- -lished in health -

September-October 1890.

49

Chapter 4

Miss Johnson treads the boards!

"The weather this year has been preternaturally unfavourable," said Miss Johnson in her first report to parents at the end of the Autumn Term, 1888. This may help to account for at least some of the increase in illness at the school. There were colds and coughs, headaches and neuralgia, backache and sore throats. And it wasn't just the pupils who were suffering: one parent complained about lessons missed "through teachers falling ill". The logbook entries for that year also remind us that some diseases which we have almost forgotten about were still a threat at the end of the nineteenth century. One child had worms, another had to be kept away because "cook has a mild form of diphtheria" while another was suffering from a weak throat as a result of scarlet fever.

Parental anxieties about the impact of school on their daughters' well-being continued. Permission was sought for one pupil to be allowed "to rest occasionally" and for another to stay away from school after 12 o'clock "in order to keep her in good health" — but, curiously, not on Friday afternoons. More concerning was the request for a child to stay at home for a term because "she worries so about lessons and is not well". Not surprisingly there were still some accusations being made. One mother called to say that the doctor had recommended gymnastic exercises for her daughter Jessie because she was "not straight" — adding that it was the fault of "these desks and high schools"! Another complained about her daughter catching a cold because windows were open in the classroom—"five minutes on account of smoke," added Miss Johnson tartly in parentheses! It is strange to think that in such a relatively recent period draughts were still believed to be a major cause of colds.

The difficulty of getting to school on time was also raised. The journeys could be quite complicated. Katie Kenyon, for instance, who lived some five miles from the school, recalled travelling with her friends Bertha Crossley and Ethel Scrimgeour. "We went by train, I from Farnworth and the other two from Moses Gate, to Trinity Street Station, and then by a horse-drawn bus which started from Holden's cab yard. The bus was helped up St. George's Road hill by an extra horse, which would be hitched on at the Junction of Marsden Road and St. George's Road. I think the bus only went as far as the Crofters and we walked from there."

One parent, unconnected with the three girls just mentioned, complained that their daughter had found the long walk trying during the bad weather while another was quite irate that Miss Johnson had "scolded" her children for being late when they couldn't help it. While the fear of being told off for lateness was almost part of school lore the length and breadth of the land, the inverted commas around the word "scolded" suggest that Miss Johnson rejected this description of her behaviour. In fact, her pupils seem to have remembered her as being very kind.

As the Headmistresses and staff of the new girls' day schools were inevitably fairly inexperienced it is clear that most of them did indeed feel the need for a strong framework of rules—particularly as they were dealing with significant numbers of children for whom the routines and requirements of day school education were quite outside all previous experience.

While we do not have a list of rules specific to 1888, one does exist from a few years later, the most notable features of which are: strict silence on the stairs, orderly behaviour on the corridors, no communication between pupils in lessons, desks not to be opened without permission, no waiting for each other outside the playground gates and no standing about the roads on the way to and from school. Order marks were given for "gross disobedience and serious moral offences".

7. Every Pupil must keep a pen, pencil and ruler, fit for use, on her desk, during lessons Desks may not be opened during a lesson except with permission.

8. Pupils going from one class-room to another must walk in line, keeping to the right, and must preserve strict silence.

9. Pupils may not wait for each other outside the playground gates, nor may they walk in groups, nor stand about the roads on their way to or from School.

10. A written excuse must be brought in every case of absence or unprepared work. No excuse, except that of illness, is accepted for unprepared work.

11. Pupils may not absent themselves from School, except in case of illness, without special permission. A written note, stating the grounds for absence, signed by parent or guardian, must be brought not later than the previous day, if such leave is required. Requests for leave of absence from Afternoon School may be made by a verbal message through the Pupil, the reason for the request being stated ; a written note must, in this case, be sent next morning.

A breach of Rule 11 renders a Pupil liable to the loss of two places in Form.

Order marks are given for gross disobedience and serious moral offences.

How strict the rules actually were in 1888 is not clear, although they do not seem to have loomed particularly large. Certainly Winifred Haslam, the daughter of Mary and William Haslam who were among the foremost members of the founding body, maintained that there were very few rules. Possibly the regime was more liberal than some, hence the demand of one father that

Miss Johnson deal with his daughter "strictly" because of a disappointing report and lack of progress.

A scolding can produce some unexpected results, however, as we can see when a Mrs Whittaker notified Miss Johnson that her daughter would be leaving school as she thought she was not a favourite because another girl had been "scolded more than she for writing a note during examination". In fact the tendency of parents to express their displeasure by serving "notice" that they were going to remove their child from school seems to have been quite common—although in many cases the threat was withdrawn once tempers had cooled.

Whatever the nature and tone of the various communications, Miss Johnson made it clear in her end-of-year report to parents that such contacts were invaluable—after all, she said, the parent has a far greater opportunity of assessing the impact that school is having on their child than the teacher. "I never feel that I know a child until I have 'talked her over' well with her mother and I hope that no one will hesitate to call or write about even the smallest point connected with their children for fear of being troublesome."

To further encourage parental involvement, particularly in the choice of subjects that a child should pursue, she expressed abhorrence of the kind of school which ground its pupils through a "rigid system" regardless of parents' wishes. "It is our effort as much as possible to individualise," she said, "to try to find out what each child is capable of and to help it to be more capable." Such comments speak volumes for her enlightened, caring approach—as does the remark that the lack of increase in pupil numbers during her first year was "not altogether to be regretted as it has enabled us to become very thoroughly acquainted with the children that we have with us."

This concern for her pupils is also borne out in her comments on "lessons", a term which, at Bolton High School for Girls at least, referred to homework. Having made it quite clear to parents and pupils that no-one should spend more than the allotted time on homework—provided that the time was conscientiously filled—Miss Johnson asked that parents sign their daughter's homework as a guarantee that only the specified time had been spent on it. In a further attempt to cut down on work she was determined to limit the number of subjects studied, adding that her belief was "that no more than two languages can be properly learnt during an ordinary school career."

Drill was an important part of the school day but Miss Johnson went further, enthusiastically promoting the value of outdoor play. She pointed out that even the most perfect system of drill could never be "a substitute for the natural running about and development of muscle and graceful movement which is brought about by healthy outdoor games." In this she may well have been influenced by memories of her father enthusiastically joining in with his pupils' games and cricket on Parker's Piece in Cambridge. Whatever the source of her commitment to outdoor exercise it is clear that she believed wholeheartedly that "all work and no play makes Jill a dull girl".

Katie Kenyon recalled drill and outdoor games with pleasure. It appears to have been Miss Jarvis who was largely responsible for these lessons. With her red-gold hair and dresses of Liberty serge in blue, green and golden-brown she must have made a striking impression in the drill hall! Katie pointed out that there were no such things as gym slips or school uniforms in those days and so the girls usually "wore out" their Sunday frocks at school and drilled and played games in them. "We played hockey with light ash sticks on the play ground behind the school," she recalled. "It was covered with gravel and sometimes stones flew about as well as the ball." With gravel flying and long dresses flapping around their ankles it must have been quite a sight, not to mention an activity fraught with danger!

But what of the quality of the teaching and learning at the start of Miss Johnson's second Spring Term? The school had been inspected by Mr T H Attwater MA of Pembroke College at the beginning of January. In the conclusion to his Inspection Report, which was submitted to the Secretary of the Local Examinations and Lectures Syndicate on January 14th 1889, he expressed the opinion that "much sound good work has been done at the School during the past year and that, where weak spots exist, they can be strengthened by means of a very little extra care."

Fifty-four girls had been examined, the lowest class orally and the older girls by written papers. Three subjects came off particularly well. Literature "had not only been admirably taught but had excited the interest of the students" while it was clear that in teaching Grammar "no pains had been spared to develop an intelligent understanding of the subject." Equally highly praised was Mathematics: "In Algebra the work was thoroughly sound and good. In Arithmetic all classes passed a very good examination. The Mathematical teaching of the School is in my judgment all that could be wished."

Regrettably, there were some low points. Marks for Geography were "exceedingly poor", the result of very scanty knowledge and the "most astonishing mistakes" being made even by girls in the upper classes. Probably even more disappointing for Miss Johnson, who only a few weeks earlier had said to parents that she had "given rather special attention and extra time to French", was the dismal performance in that subject. The girls were apparently unable to handle the tenses of even the most familiar verbs such as "savoir", "venir" and "lire" and were, consequently, unable to translate even simple sentences into French. "An attempt should seriously be made to remedy this weakness," Mr Attwater concluded.

It is possible that some of the "fault" lay with Miss Johnson's approach to the teaching of modern languages which she described as going beyond lessons that were simply "narrowly and commercially practical". Instead her priority seems to have been to enable her pupils "to get at and appreciate the thoughts and feelings of a person of a different nationality from our own". Unfortunately more grammatical rigour and translation practice were what Mr Attwater had clearly been hoping for.

If Miss Johnson were likely to be disheartened by the occasional negative aspects of this report, there were many brighter moments in that school year to raise her spirits. One was a particularly welcome gift to the cash-strapped school—the handsome present of sixty-eight volumes of "well selected books" consisting of stories, poems, biographies and travel writing which would form the nucleus of the pupils' library. Referring to this gift in her Speech Day report to parents Miss Johnson said, "I am not ashamed to beg where my girls are concerned." It must have helped a great deal, however, that the publishing company she approached was that of Macmillan, the family to whom she was so closely related!

Another heartening aspect was the fact that so many former pupils were sufficiently fond of their old school to come back in considerable numbers for the lectures and musical and dramatic entertainments that were laid on. Their marked enthusiasm resulted in plans for an alumnae association which, in Miss Johnson's words, "would have a beneficial effect in keeping up the public spirit of both past and present members." The idea was clearly well received: twenty-three former pupils turned up for the inaugural meeting in the Spring Term—which was quite impressive given how small the school still was.

In November the minutes of the governors' meeting also noted that "several entertainments are arranged for the girls to take part in this term, consisting of music and recitation". Parents were to be invited, of course—although it is doubtful whether the two fathers who had just refused to subscribe towards the cost of a "platform for entertainment" were likely to turn up! Thankfully, it would take more than a few uncooperative parents to make Miss Johnson change her mind about introducing such events into the school calendar—after all, her passion for "entertainments" was firmly rooted, stemming as it did from the Christmases of her childhood when the family used to act out scenes from Shakespeare. Apparently her sister Lucy's thrilling portrayal of Lady Macbeth sleepwalking, complete with bedroom candlestick, was legendary.

In fact Miss Johnson's willingness to perform for her pupils was one of the reasons for her great popularity. Winifred Haslam, for one, loved the way that she played the piano for the girls as they marched round the "big room". Fanny Smethurst, meanwhile, recalled how "occasionally at school parties the staff would act charades for us and on one very memorable occasion they did some scenes from 'David Copperfield' and it was the greatest joy to us to see Miss Johnson and Miss Jarvis as Dora's two aunts, and Miss Berry as David's bibulous landlady." Commenting that her Headmistress was certainly not prim, Winifred Haslam added to this picture by approvingly noting that these dramatic exploits were not confined to school for, on the occasion of one of her mother's "At Homes", Miss Johnson, Miss Jarvis and Miss Berry had entertained the assembled company in the roles of the Three Witches from "Macbeth".

While their performance may well have caused a stir, their presence at such a gathering would have come as no surprise to anybody: all three women had become firm friends of the Haslam family and in particular of

Sixth Form Group, Whitsuntide 1892.

Although taken three years later, this photo features many of the girls
who are mentioned both in this and subsequent chapters.

Back Row: Mabel Horrocks, Bertha Hewitt, Ethel Scrimgeour.
Second Row: Bessie Talbot, Katie Kenyon,
Annie Lunn, Fanny Smethurst.
Third Row: Linda Haselden, Miss Jarvis, Miss Johnson, Lucy Wilding,
Maggie Barber.

Winifred's mother Mary who regarded the trio as "beacons in the dim culture of Bolton".

There were some altogether more ambitious school productions, as well, involving casts of pupils and staff. Fanny Smethurst who was quite young at the time remembered playing two parts in "Julius Caesar". As a herald, she carried a banner emblazoned with SPQR and had to scream when Caesar was stabbed—"how we enjoyed that bit!" Her other part was that of a messenger who had to enter at the end of Anthony's oration over Caesar's dead body and give him a message. "The part of Anthony was taken by Miss Johnson herself and you can imagine my horror when I forgot to come in and Miss Johnson came out, took hold of me by the ear and dragged me on to the stage! I was so petrified with fright that I couldn't speak and she had to go on without me!" Meanwhile, Katie Kenyon, who played Casca, remembered that the girl who played Brutus was "severely reprimanded because she handled her dagger as if it were a dainty paper knife!"

While such activities were clearly very thrilling for Miss Johnson's young charges, things were scarcely less exciting behind the scenes, with significant changes in the pipeline. A proposal had been made the previous November to open a Preparatory and Kindergarten class for children under the age of eight and, despite concerns that there were only "six promises of pupils" by the following February, the project was given the go-ahead. A month later, Miss Johnson recommended to the governors that they appoint a Miss Winckler as its teacher. No doubt one of her attractions was that she was also able to teach German to the older pupils.

We also begin to find references to the uncertainty about the school's continuing tenancy of the Hopefield site— the rising cost of the rent and the lack of a large assembly room being significant drawbacks—and to the fact that the governors had already had plans drawn up for new premises. However, by August 1st, when Mr Haslam was in a position to show the governing body a revised set of plans prepared by local architects Messrs Bradshaw and Gass, the original cost had risen considerably, from £1,500 to £2,200. A request was therefore put to the agents of Hopefield for the school to continue its tenancy at a reduced rental—giving the governors until the following September to consider the implications of the revised estimate and to have alternative plans drawn up.

Naturally, the pupils themselves would not have been aware of these worries. Instead that Summer Term would forever be associated in their minds with the invitation to the whole school to a picnic at Greenthorne, the Edgworth home of the Barlows who were school governors. "We went in wagonettes," Katie Kenyon recalled, "took the tea with us and had it on the moors behind the house." The memory is such a fond one that we can assume that, for once, the moors above Bolton were bathed in sunshine!

It is perhaps appropriate to end the account of Miss Johnson's first full year by drawing attention to one of her most strongly held beliefs which had been highlighted in her report to parents at a gathering the previous December. One of the key objects of education, she had said, was to train girls to be "useful, serviceable women". Indeed, in the short time she had been at the school she had already inspired her pupils to spend their time making toys and clothes to send to the Children's Home at Edgworth, to Bolton Infirmary and even to the London Children's Hospital.

So important to her were these notions of usefulness and service that she returned to them at the end of her address, linking service firmly to moral character. She pointed out that, while not all pupils could play a conspicuous part in the musical and dramatic offerings of that evening, there wasn't a single girl who had not helped in whatever way she could. She then added, "At these times, when we see children in undress, as it were, we often catch glimpses of virtues which are hidden during the ordinary school routine. And surely, however much educational reformers may differ about this or that, we shall never get beyond the great principle that he who loves and cares to serve his fellowman has attained the very first of virtues."

April. Mother & father complain about Scripture teaching being too "superstitious" & worthless & that she had better perh. be withdrawn from the lessons —

April. Father anscious abt her progress & that she shd prepare for Coll. Of Precep-tors or Locals — with a view to going to College!

Summer Term 1892.

Ap.26th Notice because of headaches.

Ap.29th Notice —

Ap.29th Father writes, wishing her to be pushed on in Eucl. & Algebra — to begin a Latin author & to learn Eng. Grammar! I propose an interview —

April 1892.

Chapter 5

The one thing needful

By the September of 1889, there were sixty-five children in the school, an increase of eleven—ten of whom were in the new Kindergarten. In her address to parents the following December Miss Johnson explained that the "object of the Kindergarten is to lay the foundations of knowledge on the soundest principles from the very beginning; boys and girls from three years old are amused and kept thoroughly happy and at the same time their minds are prepared, 'ploughed' as it were, to receive the future seed of knowledge." Another contributory factor to the pleasantness of their experience was that each child had a "mother" in the Sixth Form—a provision which seems very forward-thinking indeed. William Haslam, who joined the Kindergarten a few years later, also recalled that all the little ones were greeted with a kiss—though it is not clear whether this was part of the teacher's job description from the outset!

Better though the pupil numbers were, Miss Johnson clearly felt that such a school not only needed, but also should be able, to attract more pupils. In the same address she pointedly remarked that "it is difficult with small numbers at the present fees to maintain a staff large enough to meet all the requirements. A town of over 100,000 inhabitants ought, I think, to be able to support a High School of at least 100 children." Winifred Haslam remembered much talk about the High School at home and thought that her parents had to come to the rescue financially at one point. She recalled that the school always insisted on paying generous salaries to the teachers and that, in those early days, there were never enough pupils to make it pay properly. "We were promised a holiday when we got to a hundred (pupils) but we never did!"

Possibly one of the problems for the school lay in public perception. In a letter written some eighteen months later, Mrs Haslam acknowledged that "over and over again through these years we have been told by candid friends that if we had less pronounced Unitarianism amongst the managers we should be more popular." She added that "we have done our utmost from time to time to widen our committee." But it takes time to alter attitudes and it is unlikely to have been the only factor in the difficulties of recruitment.

Having admitted a girl to the school the next priority was to ensure that she remained for a significant number of years. Consequently, Miss Johnson devoted much of her address to the benefits of girls staying on beyond the age of sixteen. The tendency to leave at that point, or even earlier, was a common problem in girls' day schools of the time. Many pupils, some of whom had probably not had any serious education until the age of thirteen or even later, left school for good after less than two years—just at the point where they might "derive the fullest benefit by remaining" and begin to "taste the real delights of learning". While accepting that there were inevitably circumstances which left pupils little choice but to leave at sixteen, Miss Johnson was clearly disappointed when the only reason given was that "it was 'about time' that so and so left school".

There were also very practical considerations to be taken into account. "Every girl," Miss Johnson said, "should look forward to the possibility that she may have to earn her own living." Cutting across some cosy assumptions, she pointed out that family fortunes could not be relied on and that no girl should depend on there being sufficient funds to support her if she remained single. Nor could any girl be certain of marriage, she said, and "even marriage does not always mean being provided for without exertion". Consequently, girls had to take the possibility of future employment seriously and, as every profession or occupation required a sound educational background, Miss Johnson implored fathers "not to grudge an extra year or two at the end of a girl's school life." Girls who had stayed on at school, she added, would be unlikely to turn into "idle women, mere cumberers of the ground."

But the issue was not merely a practical one: it was, for Miss Johnson, also one of mental readiness for learning. Having passed the "giggling and self-conscious" years, a girl of seventeen would be ready, she hoped, to enter upon the thoughtful stage: to wonder about her place in the world, to become acquainted "with all the best that has been said and done by all the mighty dead and living" and to acquire a taste for all that is "lovely in books or art or nature". By combining knowledge with reverence for the unknown such a girl might become, she said, not a bluestocking but—in Wordsworth's memorable phrase—"a perfect woman, nobly planned to warn, to comfort and command".

There were also other benefits to be derived from retaining the older and most able pupils as we can see from the fact that, at the start of the academic year, the governors had approved the appointment of two pupils, Ethel Haselden and Laura Brackenbury, as Student Teachers. The daughter of a Wesleyan minister, twenty-two-year-old Laura would, by the end of the academic year, have been offered a place at Newnham—the first pupil of the school to achieve this distinction. Her first year at university was also destined to be considerably eased thanks to the generous gift from an anonymous local donor of a scholarship worth £75—a considerable sum in those days.

Obviously the offer of a university place was not achieved without passing the required examinations. In 1863, following a relentless campaign by Emily Davies, one of the great pioneers of girls' education, Cambridge University had permitted schoolgirls to take their local examinations for the first time. This was very much in the nature of an experiment, and one which was not universally approved of. There were fears that girls would find the examinations too stressful, that they would suffer from too much "mental excitement" and might, heaven forbid, become vain. In fact, girls suffered no ill effects at all or at least no more than they could cope with.

In 1878, Miss Johnson's sister Alice had gained her place at Newnham on the basis of her performance in the Cambridge Senior Local Examinations. While she was at Miss Haddon's school in Dover her brother George had written an amusingly fanciful letter to her, likening the examinations she was about to sit to a host of locusts "daily drawing nearer and looking bigger" as they flew by night from Cambridge to Dover. He shows a tender concern for his sister but it seems that he need not have worried—Alice coped admirably with the "locusts"!

Bearing this in mind, Miss Johnson can have had few qualms about entering her pupils for the examinations and, as ever, her approach was sensible as we can see from her comment to parents that December. Having defended the increasing need for examinations on the basis that they provided a "proof of capacity" she laid to rest any fears about overwork saying "Cram can be avoided if plenty of time is given to the pupil to reach the required standard and by time I do not mean hours of a day, nor days of week but years of life."

Laura Brackenbury was clearly a pupil for whom examinations posed few difficulties, but what of the performance of the rest of the school? Well, on December 16th Mr Attwater delivered his verdict that "while there were two or three weak points there was also much that was very good indeed, and taking the school as a whole it has in my judgment more than maintained its position during the past year".

The "two or three weak points" must have put a considerable dampener on the overall report, however. One of these was French, where the problems of the previous year persisted. "Grammar left much to be desired in point of accuracy and knowledge. Tenses of verbs were given with much looseness, and there was a lack of acquaintance with even the commoner idioms." However, the situation was retrieved to some extent when Mr Attwater reported that two senior students had done good papers in French Literature and Composition, "the latter being decidedly successful". The good standard of work in German also introduced a more positive linguistic note into the report but the praise came with a sting in the tail when Mr Attwater added that the results were "much better than in French".

Mathematics, meanwhile, continued to be something of a beacon, with Mr Attwater going so far as to say that "I have rarely examined a school which has done better in Algebra." Gratifyingly, a number of girls had successfully tackled a higher paper of "considerable difficulty". History, too, had been ably taught resulting in many papers that were "far above average". Geography, however, remained firmly in the doldrums being described as "weak all through". "Even among the senior girls," lamented Mr Attwater, "most extraordinary blunders appear." Similarly forthright comments dealt a blow to the teaching of Grammar too where the pupils' ability to parse and analyse sentences was judged to be "poor in the extreme".

A mere four days later, Miss Johnson made what was possibly one of the first changes to be prompted by Mr Attwater's report. Homework, then as now, was vital to the success of any individual pupil, yet "home-lessons" were, as Miss Johnson acknowledged, the great "crux" of a day school. Unsupervised, younger children found it particularly difficult to spend the proper amount of time on the work and to do it effectively. Miss Johnson, therefore, introduced some changes: the hours devoted to afternoon prep in school were to be extended and it was to become a rule for lower school children that they must, as far as possible, attend the sessions. Thus the need for taking any books home would be minimised and their homework would be properly supervised.

Miss Johnson assured the parents that her staff were more than happy to take on this additional burden of supervision. It is to be hoped that they really were!

General Knowledge Exam

I. What is a map? Draw a map of the way you would walk from the Lancashire and Yorkshire Railway Station to the High School, marking names of the streets you would pass through.

II. Write briefly what you know of the following persons – (1) Sir George Tryon (2) Lobengula (3) Lord Rosebery (4) Nansen (5) Duke of York (6) Louis Kossuth.

III. If it is clear will Jupiter be visible this evening? At what times of the year are the Great Bear & Orion visible in Bolton?

Make a picture of the stars in these constellations.

IV. Explain the meaning of the following expressions-to weigh anchor, to box the compass, to board ship, to scuttle a boat, to weather a gale, to ship a sea, to raise a siege, to lead the van.

V. What do you understand by a "strike?

VI. Distinguish between the meaning of the following words: (1) bootless & shoeless (2) numeration & enumeration (3) borough & burrow (4) satire & satyr (5) libel & label (6) irritate & irrigate (7) stationery & stationary.

VII. Who killed Cock Robin?

VIII. What is "following on" in cricket? Why is it a topic of discussion at present?

IX. Describe the picture which hangs in the middle of the wall opposite the platform in the Assembly room.

X. In what direction is New Zealand? What are its native inhabitants called? Do their heads point upwards as ours do?

XI. Where are the following places? Write shortly anything you know about them:
(1) Bulawayo (2) Ubbazia (3) the Old Kent Road (4) Siam (5) Georgetown (6) Uganda (7) the Box Tunnel (8) Chicago.

A typical internal General Knowledge Exam from the period.

Any attempt to further address the issues raised by the Inspection must have been seriously compromised by what appears to have been an unusually high level of long-term illness in the Spring Term. By late January most of the entries in Miss Johnson's log relate to lengthy absences: one pupil was not going to return to school until the end of winter, another who had suffered from headaches since the age of ten was leaving altogether, while a third pupil was not returning until after Whitsuntide and a fourth might "perhaps" return after summer. Some pupils battled on but were to do no afternoon work or were to be excused from homework. This must have been disappointing, particularly after Miss Johnson had expressed satisfaction, in the previous term, that about a third of the pupils were regularly attending the town gymnasium and had "wonderfully improved in looks and health".

Occasionally, Miss Johnson's comments suggest a level of irritation that we have not seen before. Pointing out that her daughter had fainted in Arts and Crafts, one mother requested that she was not to be "urged" as her health was "not yet established". Next to the word "fainted" Miss Johnson added "feint" in brackets. Then there was the case of a father who wrote to remind Miss Johnson that they had discussed the propriety of his daughter being out of doors after measles. At the end of this entry Miss Johnson added "cock and bull story" in brackets.

Most concerning of all, however, is the entry for February 21st which notes that a pupil had died on February 17th. "Her mother says she was 'persecuted' at school," the entry continues. The only other reference to this tragic case comes in the minutes of the governors' meeting for March 5th when it was agreed that one half of the school fee and the whole of the fee for piano lessons should be returned to the parents as the child in question had attended school on only three days of the term. There is no further explanation of what the persecution might have been, whether it contributed to her death or whether, indeed, the accusation was justified.

Interestingly quite a number of parental requests were met with a flat refusal. These included a request for a child to drop Algebra, a request for another to learn "Arithmetic instead of Algebra because it will be 'more useful'!" and two from a Mrs Macbeth—firstly that her daughter should go up a class and secondly that she should learn German instead of Latin. Possibly it was the idea of replacing Latin with German that caused a problem, as Miss Johnson allowed another pupil to take up German, provided that she waited until Christmas. It may well be that she was influenced by her grandfather's views on this: he had held that "the study of the Classics is, on the whole, advantageous to public morals, by inspiring an elegance of sentiment and an elevation of soul, which we should in vain seek for elsewhere."

Parental input of a different kind, however, was clearly very welcome: in her December address Miss Johnson had publicly thanked parents for the kind loan of books, plants and microscopes as well as curtains and props for "our little dramatic attempts". Two parents had organised a trip to the Tyldesley coal mine, Mr Haslam had taken a party round his spinning mills and weaving sheds and the Reverend Brackenbury had given a lecture on John Wesley. Miss Johnson also took the opportunity to thank her own father—whom she modestly described as "a schoolmaster of some forty years' standing"—for visiting the school and giving "a little talk about the organs of speech". Committed to encouraging ever greater parental involvement she then made an offer which seems very modern indeed—parents, she said, were welcome to "visit on any working day and hear some lessons given."

As regards future plans, it is clear that a site on Park Road was being considered for the new school. A proposal was made in the November to set up a Limited Company which would help to fund the building and it was agreed that parents and other interested parties should be invited to a meeting on December 16th to consider the scheme. The following February the school was given notice to terminate occupation of Hopefield on 1st September 1890 when the lease expired, which prompted a request for a further six months' tenancy and "month by month tenancy beyond that, if required by the school".

On a lighter note, there was also some discussion of the enticing prospect of "an exhibition of handwork of various kinds done by past and present scholars and, in connection with it, a garden party and athletic sports" to take place on July 12th. As in the previous year, Miss Johnson was given £5 to spend on the event. As well as Swedish Drill, Ball Exercises, and a Potato Race there would be Recitations from the Lower and Upper Schools. The event was also to include displays of Needlework, Art, Flowers, Cookery and, for those with an inclination for such things, there was to be a competition in pencil sharpening. Finally Mr Morris's band was to be engaged to play a selection of music during the afternoon.

How very different Miss Johnson was from her schoolmaster grandfather who had been rather wary about Drawing, Music and other such "subordinate" accomplishments, even going so far as to say that "a passion for Music is very ensnaring, and peculiarly calls for self control"! With at least two events each year which allowed pupils to demonstrate their physical, artistic and performance skills—not to mention their abilities in helping with all the preparations—Miss Johnson clearly felt that such activities were a crucial part of education, particularly if they allowed a child who was not especially academic to shine.

Her own words on this are revealing: "It goes without saying that no parent thinks her child without ability and we teachers ought to take the same point of view, I believe, if we are to produce the best results. The ability or faculty that each child possesses may often lie quite outside the ordinary routine of lessons and when that ordinary routine is interrupted for a moment we get the chance of finding out what the special faculty of each child is. For when she knows the 'one thing' she can do really well that is for her 'the one thing needful'."

The proposal for the exhibition and garden party was minuted at the governors' meeting on Wednesday May 7th but any pleasure at the prospect of the event must have been gravely tempered by the news that Mr Isaac Barrow, a governor and one of the school's earliest and staunchest supporters, had died suddenly that very day. The governors placed on record "their sense of the great loss they have sustained in the decease of Mr Isaac Barrow who since the commencement of the School has been a most able, generous and constant worker in its behalf. (They) would bear grateful testimony to the value of the long and quiet help so freely rendered."

Sadly, there must have been a number of other deaths in the school community that year for, in her December address to parents, Miss Johnson had observed that "we cannot meet together here this evening without recalling how many faces we had hoped to see whom we miss tonight and whom we shall never see again—especially our dear little one, whose recitation last year 'Oh call my brother back to me' comes back to us now as if it had been almost prophetic." It is impossible at this distance in time to know what the sad event was to which this poignant comment referred.

Sep. 20ᵗʰ Provisional notice –
(going to boarding-school)
answered.

Sep. 26ᵗʰ Notice – (no cause)

Sep. 26ᵗʰ To discontinue piano-les
sons without notice –

Sep. 26ᵗʰ ∴ We break our contract –

Sep. 26ᵗʰ Notice – & to leave off
music –

Sep. 26ᵗʰ Absent for term on accᵗ
of health.

Sep. 26ᵗʰ Absent for health for the
present –

Sep. 26ᵗʰ 16 – Has been at C.I. not
developed for her age – or
musical to her father's disappointment – To go finally
abroad & get rid of prejudices!

Sep. 26ᵗʰ Father writes (unknown to
mother) to complain of "stooping"
probably due to wrong-sized
desk & of "flip-flop"
Arithc teaching – I reply –
Mother opens my letter &
apologises – thinks Annie
is perh: being taken on too
fast – She is to learn Drilling

September 1892.

Chapter 6

Juggling home and school

The opening of the new school building on Park Road was arguably the most significant event not only in the school's history up to that point but also of Miss Johnson's headship.

However, at the start of the school year in September 1890 it was by no means certain when the move would take place. In October, the governing body had to negotiate a further six months' tenancy at Hopefield and, should it be required, month by month after that but at an increased rent. With the prospect of higher charges the governors must have been more than a little anxious for the new school to be ready and clearly the teaching staff were no less impatient. According to Miss Johnson it was the one absorbing topic of interest during that academic year—the constantly repeated remark being, "Such and such a thing shall be done when we get in the new school."

Meanwhile the day-to-day business of the school ran on. Joining the staff, probably as a replacement for Miss Jackson, was Miss Maude Horner who had been educated at Croydon High School in the period when Miss Johnson taught there. There was also a new assistant for the teaching staff in the form of Alice Brackenbury. Already a pupil of the school, Alice had been appointed as a Student Teacher in place of her sister Laura who had just started at Newnham. There had also been a gratifying increase in pupil numbers and, when she looked back over the school year some months later, Miss Johnson was able to praise the regularity of attendance—despite the difficulties caused by the weather, especially on one very stormy November day when forty-two per cent of the pupils were absent.

The weather was probably not entirely to blame for the fact that a number of pupils were suffering from quite serious health problems: one child had a weak heart, another very delicate child was suffering from congestion of the lungs while a third had had two "attacks of palpitation" which had prompted her mother to request that she "avoid drill and standing to answer". Coming as she did from a family plagued by health problems, Miss Johnson would almost certainly have treated such cases with great sympathy. However, when a letter about a minor ailment contained a veiled accusation, she was quite capable of making an acerbic reply: "October 24th: Mother writes she has a bad cold and sore throat, probably increased by going out in the (school) garden at playtime—in *thin* shoes, I say."

For the first time there seem to have been as many general complaints as there were letters about health. These included the predictable objections to "unfavourable" report comments, three of which resulted in the pupil in question being withdrawn. The mother of one of these children objected strongly to the implication that her daughter was not doing well at school as a result of having too many chores to do at home. She immediately went along to confront Miss Johnson, stating emphatically that her daughter had no home duties and pointing the finger of blame at the school: if anything was responsible for her lack of progress, she said, it was that she spent far too long reading novels! The parent of one of the other pupils in question, while agreeing that her daughter was difficult, still wanted her to leave because she "dislikes being laughed at (by mistress) and thinks she should have more marks if she does more work".

Not all reactions were hostile, however. One mother wrote to promise that her daughter would "try to get over the sulks" while a Mr Dowson was pleased with the report and hoped that his daughter would "learn to keep silence". Meanwhile a Mrs Warbrick expressed disappointment rather than anger about a comment that her daughter was not conscientious, to which Miss Johnson replied: "She is only careless about keeping rules."

In fact, Miss Johnson was the first to accept the difficulty many girls experienced in obeying school rules and regulations to the letter, particularly if such requirements were quite new to them. Still, she and her staff expected a high standard of conduct and, while pointing out that "it is our rule here not to offer the incentive of material rewards and prizes", she had instigated a system of little gilt stars the previous year. These were to be given to "those who have climbed the 'starry heights' of virtue, to whose conduct as schoolgirls no single blame has been attached during the whole term".

One of the chief virtues that Miss Johnson expected of her pupils was that of humility. No child was to make a distinction between herself and another on the basis of class and all pupils were expected to be friendly with each other regardless of background. She was not unusual in this as all the new day schools subscribed to the same philosophy. But many middle class parents genuinely feared that only negative effects would flow from their daughters mixing with those lower down the social ladder. Many people were simply not ready for more egalitarian notions.

How great the potential was for genuine social mixing is not clear as the only list we have of parental occupations comes from a decade earlier, when managerial and professional roles dominated. However, all the evidence suggests that it was probably not very different in Miss Johnson's time—the fathers of the three girls whose reminiscences feature in this book being a good indication. William Kenyon was a manufacturer of cotton goods, Charles Smethurst was an exporter of cotton yarn and William Haslam owned the Haslam Spinning Company. These were all positions of significance in a town and county famously responsible for supplying cotton goods to the world. But of course there were some girls from far less privileged backgrounds in the school, as we can see when one pupil complained that Miss Johnson had tried to make her more friendly with scholarship girls. "She evidently felt the possession of wealth was a special reason for public spirit," the child in question observed, clearly unconvinced.

While the odd pupil may have openly resented such liberal sentiments from Miss Johnson, there is no evidence of parents overtly challenging her on this. Rather their complaints arise from normal playground boisterousness or childish lack of common sense. One pupil had apparently gone home feeling sick after being "swung around" at play-time while another young child had arrived home on a cold day wearing "only her mackintosh and *carrying* her jacket on her arm" — this was coupled with a comment about the kindergarten children "quarrelling over their dressings". More bizarrely, a regular aspect of every school day became the unexpected source of annoyance for one parent who objected to the fact that the school provided dinners!

Unlike boarding schools, day schools were very likely to encounter problems when home life and school routines did not sit easily together. A Mrs Wallwork requested that her children's music lessons should be at a time which did not interfere with dinners, because the family had breakfast very early. Not unconnected was the difficulty of the journey to and from school for some pupils. School finished at 12.55 and Ethel Scrimgeour's mother wrote in to say that her daughter had to hurry to catch the train at 1.40. Katie Kenyon had similar difficulties; she recalled that, by the time she had changed from her indoor shoes and done up her high-laced or buttoned boots, she was left with little time to catch her train or horse-drawn bus. Maybe footwear was also the source of Ethel's difficulties!

Transport was a troublesome issue at many of the new girls' day schools. Consequently, those schools that had the option to do so often chose to locate themselves in quiet suburbs so that their pupils were able to walk to and from their lessons, thereby avoiding the "moral and social danger" of public transport. Then, by the last decade of the century, another solution was beginning to emerge when some schools started to provide their own transport. There is no indication, however, that Bolton High School for Girls offered any such facility in Miss Johnson's time.

William Heywood Haslam, youngest son of William and Mary Haslam
and brother of Winifred,
shortly after his flowing curls had been cut.

For some, however, travel was not quite so difficult. Katie Kenyon recalled how the children of John Percival Haslam arrived in "governess carriages" every morning, each pony carriage overflowing with children. "The youngest member of the family was a beautiful little boy exactly like the pictures of Little Lord Fauntleroy," she noted. "He wore a velvet suit with a lace collar and had long curls and large blue eyes!" This captivating child was Percy Lovell Haslam who, too young for school, was probably just going along for the ride with his older sisters. Evidently his equally young cousin William Haslam was also blessed with similarly flowing locks but, in his case at least, this "misfortune" as he amusingly called it had been remedied by the time he started school—thus saving Katie from being doubly beguiled!

Despite a distinguished career in naval, diplomatic and business affairs William Haslam always claimed that his time at his first school had been "dearer to him than anything that came after".

Miss Johnson's log also testifies to a development that she must have found very gratifying: the increase in parental ambition. A Mr Thornley entered his daughter into the school with the express wish that she "be prepared for matriculation standard, especially Latin and Mathematics, with a view perhaps to a doctor's profession" while Ethel Scrimgeour's mother wanted her to prepare for Cambridge. Keen to encourage girls to seize the new opportunities with both hands, Miss Johnson was nevertheless equally attentive to girls who were struggling—for instance making the sensible suggestion that a pupil who was finding French and Scripture too much for her should go back to Form 1 and should also come to afternoon prep.

December saw not only the appointment of Miss Coombs to teach Drawing but also the third school Inspection of Miss Johnson's headship, this time under the scrutiny of Mr T Stevens MA of Magdalen College. All was well and he was able to deliver a very positive verdict: "The school is exceedingly well looked after and in excellent order, the teaching throughout conscientiously distributed. The conduct and tone, so far as I could form an opinion, leave nothing to be desired."

As regards the Kindergarten, Mr Stevens was pleased to report that "the tiny children are being taught suitably to their age, school is being made pleasant as well as profitable to them." At this point it was already known that Miss Winckler was resigning her position that Christmas—"Bolton not suiting her health"—and that her replacement, Miss Kemp, was to commence in the Spring Term. It seems that Miss Winckler's health had been poor for quite some time as, a year earlier, Fannie

Jarvis's younger sister Nellie had been brought in to cover for her. A few months later the governors had approved funds to train her "in the Kindergarten system" — though why she did not become Miss Winckler's permanent replacement remains a mystery.

Miss Johnson must have also breathed a sigh of relief when she read Mr Stevens' comments about French which could not have been more different from those of the previous year: "The accent of the older pupils struck me as good, and it is clear that great care has been bestowed on Grammar, the formation of the tenses of French verbs etc. The rendering of English into French was also good, so long as it kept to the strict lines of the exercise book." English, meanwhile, received fulsome praise, with all the papers judged as being "exceedingly good", showing fair critical knowledge and a creditable grasp of unusual words and phrases.

Oddly, given the excellent reports on the teaching of mathematics up to this point, Mr Stevens warned that the pupils' grounding in the basics was not secure, many of their Arithmetic papers being "meagre and disappointing". Moreover, the lack of firm grounding in "money sums, weights and measures" was hindering their attempts to grapple with "what lies beyond", for example Vulgar and Decimal Fractions. The one depressingly predictable element of the report was that the problem with Geography persisted, with children confusing "monsoon" with "simoon" and attributing the motions of the earth to the prevailing winds!

The report also noted the growing number of successes in the higher examinations, with distinctions for Laura

Brackenbury in French and for Elizabeth Hutchinson in English. Four other girls had "satisfied" the Cambridge and Oxford Examiners and there had been some pleasing individual results in the examinations of Freehand Drawing, Physiography and Plain Needlework. Overall, then, this was a positive enough report to carry forward into 1891—the year which was dominated by the opening of the new school.

By the end of 1890 the week beginning April 6th had been earmarked for the event, and, raising excitement to fever pitch, Mrs Millicent Garrett Fawcett had "kindly consented to open the new school". One of the foremost campaigners for women's rights, she was the widow of Henry Fawcett who had been Professor of Political Economy at Cambridge as well as Liberal MP for both Brighton and Hackney and, from 1880, the Postmaster General. Her elder sister, Elizabeth Garrett Anderson, was no less distinguished. After years of fierce opposition from vested male interests, she had become Britain's first woman doctor and had gone on to found the New Hospital for Women in London—staffed entirely by women—and been elected Dean of the London School of Medicine in 1883.

Far from being in her sister's shadow, however, Millicent Fawcett was an outstanding organiser and had just been elected leader of the National Union of Women's Suffrage Societies. She was also involved in a number of other high profile campaigns, including the fight for married women's property rights. But, above all else, it was her passionate commitment to women's higher education that made her such an appropriate choice for the task of opening Park Road. In 1868 she had written an article on this subject for "Macmillan's Magazine" and had become heavily involved in organising the lectures for women which eventually led to the founding of Newnham College in 1871. In fact, her Cambridge home had been a hub for those involved in the whole Newnham venture and her help and shrewd advice were fundamental both to the setting up and later development of the college.

Engaging an eminent guest speaker was all very well but the first requirement of the much-awaited event was a completed building. We do not have the exact date when construction work had begun but Katie Kenyon remembered the morning when the whole school had walked across to Park Road to watch Miss Johnson and Bessie Warbrick, the youngest pupil, lay the first two bricks of the new building. Clearly, things were well under way by November 1890: Mr Haslam was asked to attend to the preparation of the new playground and the suggestion of early April for the grand opening was put forward. At long last people must have felt that they really could begin to turn their attention to guest lists, speech writing and the thrill of planning and rehearsing the evening's entertainment. And, as far as some of the girls at least were concerned, a major event like this meant new clothes—Winifred Haslam remembered the thrill of having a pink silk dress for the occasion and being very proud of it!

However, as is so often the case with these things, the date of the opening slipped—by a whole month. So it was not until Friday May 8th 1891 at 4.00 pm that everyone gathered to see Mrs Fawcett formally declare the new school buildings open.

Feb. 6th Mother writes to beg for special indulgence for "Grace" who is not "stupid or inattentive" but only very deaf _ and not at all well! She does not care for Annie to lie down after dinner, as I propose but wd rather she prepared lessons on wet days _ + played on fine days. Grace has headaches + is apt to cry.

Feb 10th Father writes to complain of too much home-lessons _ She was three hours (instead of 1½ hrs) over them on Thurs: eve? _ I point out that she must keep to her time _

Feb 3d. Brother calls _ says she has had trouble with her back _ + twitching in her eye _ so is not to do gymnastics at present

Feb.- "One of the elder girls" hurt her foot _

Feb. Notice _ To finish! I remonstrate _ She is to stay till summer

Feb 15th Notice _
(she is half. engaged!)

February 1893.

89

Chapter 7

Gracious souls in a beautiful habitation

Situated in a quiet location next to Queen's Park, the new school was easily accessible from all parts of the town. It was a sign of the governors' confidence in the school's future that, although current pupil numbers were in the region of eighty, the new building had been designed to accommodate 360 pupils—with room for further expansion if necessary.

The new school building, 1891.

The Bolton "Journal" described the building as picturesque. The lower part was of red brick and stone while the upper part was half-timbered with a gabled roof from which rose a series of chimneys, each one distinct in design from its neighbour. In addition to bay windows and leaded lights, there were many decorative mouldings including carved heraldic griffons, one of which bore a lozenge-shaped shield bearing the school's coat of arms—the lozenge being regarded as the "proper form for coats of arms when borne by ladies".

The accommodation itself consisted of a very large and handsome assembly room on the first floor which boasted a very striking roof of dark oak "having an arched portion in the centre and the side spandrels fitted with moulded uprights". It was hoped that the assembly room, with its splendid ceiling, leaded lights and open fireplaces would also be used by the general public for lectures, concerts and other such events. The classrooms, meanwhile, were lofty and spacious, each one placed "so as to get the most cheerful outlook and be as sunny as possible". The colours chosen for the woodwork and walls, while subtle in tone, were nonetheless different in each classroom. Quite advanced in design, each room also had an open fireplace fitted with a special "Manchester" grate, that provided not only heat but also warm fresh air, as well as outlet ventilators in the chimney breasts to "ensure specially healthy conditions".

With a view to providing the best in the way of cookery lessons for the girls, the kitchen was especially large and fitted with a very fine range. Meanwhile, the pupils' need for exercise and fresh air was catered for by the provision not only of very large playgrounds protected from the road by brick walls, but also a tennis court and grass embankments. And finally, with a nod to the wet Lancashire weather, the cloakroom was well appointed with arrangements for keeping the girls' outer clothing properly aired.

Seated in the splendid hall on that afternoon in May, the "large and fashionable gathering" settled down to a programme of prize giving and speeches. After the opening hymn and a prayer from the Reverend Canon Atkinson, the Governors' Report was read by Mr French who proudly noted that the school had made its mark and was fulfilling a most useful function in the neighbourhood by exercising "a healthful and refining influence upon our future townswomen". He then commented on the success of the Kindergarten in producing "carefully trained little people" before urging parents to allow their daughters to sit the public examinations offered by the school—on the interesting grounds that this helped the Mistresses to measure the success of their teaching against that of other schools. One of his final points was to note the significant changes to the structure of the governing body which were designed to bring in younger members who were "more abreast with the times".

Miss Johnson's report followed and it is safe to assume that, because of the very special nature of the occasion, she used the opportunity to highlight those things she valued most. From what we know of her already, it comes as no surprise that she paid special attention to the value of Arts and Crafts, linking this with the successful exhibition of the girls' work the previous summer. "The importance of hand and eye training," she said, "even for those who have not to depend on clever hands for the means of livelihood, is becoming more and more recognised by the leaders of education." One of the most important aspects of learning, she said, "(is) the knowledge which is gained by observation of concrete objects, rather than from books; and, in the direction of Art, the study so far as is possible of the best models."

Robustly defending two trips that had taken place the previous term—one to the Autumn Exhibition of Pictures in Manchester and one in which Mrs Tillotson and Mrs Brimelow had arranged for thirteen children to be shown round the Printing Office of the "Evening News"—she pointed out that, as there was comparatively little opportunity for such visits in Bolton itself, "surely none which occurs in the immediate neighbourhood should be neglected."

Returning to another familiar theme, that of parental involvement, she spoke of the special advantage that a day school has over a boarding school—the opportunity it gives to parents of knowing all about their children and of taking a strong interest in their daily pursuits during the most important period of their lives. Consequently, in the previous year, she had invited the mothers of the children in the Upper School to meet the ladies of the governing body and herself, so that they could discuss as a group any school matters they wished to raise. About twenty had turned up and by the end of the meeting Miss Johnson felt that "we should henceforth work still more harmoniously together".

Given the presence of Mrs Fawcett, not to mention her own views, the issue of women's access to university courses was bound to be mentioned. Having praised the generosity of the anonymous donation which had enabled Laura Brackenbury to proceed to Newnham College, Miss Johnson took the opportunity to thank the Hulton Trustees[10] for "making it more fully patent that a school such as ours is the direct link between the Elementary Schools and the Universities." This link had been created by the Trustees' provision not only of a scholarship each year to an Elementary School pupil but also of a newly-established Leaving Scholarship of £35 for two or three years to a pupil of seventeen or more who wished to go on to university.

The conclusion to Miss Johnson's address centred on the desire to hand down "noble traditions to future generations who shall be trained by other hands than ours". In mentioning Mr Isaac Barrow, who had died just a year earlier and who would have rejoiced to see the fruit of his labours, she linked the idea of noble traditions firmly with that of service. "It is such lives, full of service to man, that we shall hope to set before our children as examples worthy of imitation," she said. "The great lessons of a public school must ever be the lessons of sympathy and charity." Then, having thanked the architects Messrs Bradshaw and Gass for their patient attention to, and ungrudging discussion of, details, she made a promise to them that "since they

---

[10] Nathaniel Hulton, a London Salter, created the Hulton Trust in 1692, part of the income from which was to be used to pay for an annual lecture or sermon to be delivered in his native Bolton by a Protestant Minister. Some of his money was later used to endow a school in Moor Lane, Bolton. Then, during the final decade of the nineteenth century and with Charity Commission approval, the Hulton Trustees began awarding scholarships to both the Boys' Grammar School and the High School for Girls.

have made us such a beautiful habitation, we will do our best to fill it with beautiful and gracious souls."

In his role as Chairman, Professor A W Ward, Principal of Owen's College,[11] then made a plea for girls' schools to avoid the narrowness that characterised so much of boys' education. While not denying that the academic road to the professions was what many girls desired, he wished their teaching to be liberated as far as possible from the early specialisation that so often stunted a boy's learning. Instead girls' schools should seize the opportunity that their relative newness gave them to devise a curriculum that was freer, broader and more attuned to true culture pursued for its own sake.

And then it was the turn of the great Mrs Fawcett. The reporter for the Bolton "Journal" described her as a small buoyant woman attired in a most unassuming manner. Thankfully we have the recollections of Winifred Haslam who, with a girl's rather more acute eye for such things, remembered her wearing an elegant dress of grey silk. When Mrs Fawcett rose to speak she was, of course, "very cordially received and presented with a handsome bouquet". Given the nature of the occasion and of her tireless campaigning on behalf of girls' education, the warmth of her reception is scarcely surprising. However, as far as some of the girls in the audience were concerned, there was an even better reason to applaud her so vigorously—a reason noted by Professor Ward when he humorously observed that Mrs Fawcett might in the future be acclaimed almost as much for being the "mother of Philippa".

---

[11] The precursor of the University of Manchester.

The story behind this quip was that Philippa Fawcett had been placed "above the Senior Wrangler" in the Cambridge Mathematical Tripos examination of 1890. Miss Johnson herself had been in the Senate House when this outstanding achievement had been announced and, on her return to Bolton, she had given everyone a thrilling account of the event. It was an achievement guaranteed to stir the heart of any girl with aspirations to a university education—and indeed Miss Johnson and a number of the girls had sent Philippa a letter of congratulations. So it is quite likely that, in the minds of many of her young audience that afternoon, Mrs Fawcett was indeed more revered for being Philippa's mother. "Afterwards," said Katie Kenyon, "I learned to honour Mrs Fawcett for her own sake, for all her work for the higher education of women and for her untiring efforts for women's suffrage."

Her speech was strikingly modern in its sentiments. As Miss Johnson herself had done on so many occasions, Mrs Fawcett emphasised the need for "hearty co-operation" between home and school and for parents to encourage and direct their children's natural curiosity and eagerness to understand the world around them. She also argued against the type of "education" whose object was "to produce a calculating machine or a walking encyclopaedia, or a creature capable of automatic reproduction of everything that is poured into it." For her the only true object of education was to make the best of whatever faculty or talent the child might possess so as to produce good and useful citizens who would "leave the world nobler, purer, and braver for their existence in it". This was indeed a fine and lofty sentiment, and one for which she made no apology. "He who aims at a tree," she added, "will never bring down a star. We do well to aim at perfection though we know we shall never reach it."

Mrs Fawcett also used her platform to urge ever greater equality for women, arguing that the "highest mischief has been attained in those departments of human activity where women have been rigorously shut out." Referring to the early fears about the impact of education on girls, she observed that mental occupation and activity had proved not to have any "injurious effect on the physical frame, but the contrary." Women were already achieving high honours at Cambridge with neither the injury to physical development nor the vanity that some had feared. The pioneering students, she was glad to say, had done nothing to discredit the cause of women's education in this respect. "We may go on rejoicing," she concluded, "confident that the opening of the avenues of education and freedom to women has been an unmixed good."

Mrs Fawcett then declared the school open and the formal part of the proceedings drew to a close with votes of thanks, a speech of congratulations from Miss Day, the Headmistress of Manchester High School for Girls, and the hope expressed by Professor Randall of University College Liverpool that the school "might long be the nursery of gentle minds".

The day of celebration concluded with an evening soirée. Mr Morris's band played selections of music and the girls performed dramatic extracts and songs which included "The Murder of Caesar"—for once without Miss Johnson in the role of Mark Anthony—Browning's

"Strafford" and, after the interval, "Songs from Fairyland", a recitation of Christina Rossetti's "Goblin Market" and Farmer's "Nursery Rhyme Quadrilles". Everyone must have breathed a sigh of relief and satisfaction that the school had at long last been formally opened and in such style. Now all that remained was to move everything across from Hopefield over the weekend, ready for the start of school on the following Monday.

A contemporary drawing of Park Road which highlights the large and elaborately leaded windows.

Unfortunately, as is so often the case, there were one or two small flies in the ointment. Immediately after the event Mr Coe, the Minister of Bank Street Unitarian Chapel, wrote to Mrs Haslam protesting in the strongest terms against the decision to open the proceedings with the hymn "Now thank we all our God"—his objection being to the words "All praise and thanks to God the Father now be given, the Son, and Him who reigns with them in highest Heaven". "No Unitarian should countenance that," he raged, "particularly when he occupies a seat on the platform!"

Responding immediately, Mrs Haslam sprang to the defence of the hymn's propriety. She pointed out that the aim of all those who had worked over the previous fourteen years to establish a high school for girls in Bolton had been "to supply the kind of institution known by that name elsewhere"—in other words an establishment characterised by religious freedom. "To make it a Unitarian stronghold," she added, "is our last wish." Indeed her own son, William, later recalled how the daily prayers were very non-committal.

The other key reason for her determination to tackle the minister head on over his complaint was the issue of pupil numbers. Ever since the founding of the school, friends of Mary Haslam had suggested to her that pupil numbers might be greater if there were not such a widespread perception in the town that the governing body had a pronounced Unitarian bias. As strenuous efforts had been made to counter this view it is no surprise to find Mrs Haslam concluding her letter with a forthright statement of her personal commitment to tolerance and religious freedom: "Live and let live … *I* should object to my own theological views taking any precedence over those of my Wesleyan, Church and Quaker friends on that same Committee."

The second fly in the ointment was revealed in the minutes of the governors' meeting for the following June. "Owing to severe attacks of influenza which prostrated Miss Johnson and her head assistant mistress, Miss Jarvis, immediately after the opening of the new buildings, it was necessary to disperse the pupils on May 11th (instead of 14th) for the Whitsuntide Holidays and it was found needful to postpone the re-assembling of the school until June 9th (instead of June 2nd) in order to give the invalids more time for recovery."

With hindsight it is easy to see that all the stress and excitement of getting ready to move in to the new school, combined with the huge effort needed to prepare for the opening ceremony, was almost guaranteed to leave both women with little resistance to infection once they relaxed. Presumably many of the pupils rejoiced in the extra ten days' holiday but perhaps there were some at least who didn't wish to be parted from their wonderful new school for quite so long!

Feb. 20th: Mother complains of having to make so many confusing "little payments" — requests for a bill to be sent in inclusive of all these —

Mar. 2d Mother "hurt" that we have not enquired about her absence before — I explain that I thought she was taking a rest after the Music Exam"

Mar. 3d I suggest to father that she shd learn "lip speech"

Mar. 3d request that we should not order music from Parwin's for "scholars" without an official order from them!

Mar.)th Notice because mother is not strong! She is not to give up lessons altogether, but it is a pity for her to waste time on Euc. & Algebra

Mar.)th Not to be pressed with lessons on returning from her illness (typhoid before Xmas.)

February-March 1893.

101

Chapter 8

Accusations fly

After all the excitement of the move to Park Road, the first year in the new building seems to have been characterised by a greater level of parental fractiousness than normal—at least according to the Miss Johnson's log.

There were, of course, the usual health issues to cope with, ranging from deafness, tonsillitis and stiff necks to headaches, laryngitis and "growing too fast"—with some parents still very quick to claim that sitting in draughts at school had either caused or was likely to exacerbate some of the ailments. Travel remained problematic with one child being withdrawn because the journey to and from school was too long and the trams were not "select". But it wasn't just the problem of unavoidable contact with different social classes on trams and trains that was giving rise to alarm; the sheer number of vehicles on the roads was causing at least one parent to consider withdrawing her daughter.

Despite Miss Johnson's earlier attempts to nip homework concerns in the bud the matter still continued to rankle with some parents. Three complaints about homework taking too long—up to four hours in one case—were received in quick succession. The last of these placed the blame squarely on the "fear of Returned Lessons"—in other words substandard work which was returned to the pupil to be done again. That other predictable source of irritation, the school report, threw up a number of complaints from "disappointed" and "grieved" parents, including one who challenged the description of her daughter as "rough". Happily, that particular matter was speedily resolved when, after a brief discussion with Miss Johnson, the mother conceded that her daughter was indeed rough!

Even the Kindergarten was not immune from criticism. One mother bemoaned the fact that her child had not been happy since Miss Winckler left while a father refused to send his son back to school because the fee had gone up to three guineas to cover the extra hour, between 12.00 and 1pm, which had come into force at the start of term. Alarmed by this, Miss Johnson contacted the governors who promptly resolved the issue by removing the extra hour and returning the fee its previous level of two guineas. This was immediately followed by a mother threatening to take her daughter out of the Kindergarten "unless she may stay till one"!

It was not until after the Christmas break, however, that a fairly new phenomenon emerged: the tendency of parents to accuse each other's children. Once again, it would appear that day schools were particularly vulnerable to such complaints as children with very different backgrounds and standards of behaviour, relatively speaking, were thrown together in a way that simply would not have happened before. Indeed, the minutes of the governors' meetings for 1892 show only too clearly that they found the issue a difficult one: their natural desire to be as inclusive as possible was inevitably being tempered by the fear of adverse reactions from existing parents. On this particular occasion the matter had arisen when the landlord of a pub applied for a place for his daughter. After some discussion the governors decided that it was "not desirable to admit children living in Public Houses" and then added, as a concession to their naturally more liberal tendencies, "but each case was to be considered on its merits".

The first two parental complaints about undesirable children were relatively low key. One particular pupil was felt to be an unhelpful influence, though in what manner the log does not specify, while another child was accused of being so ill mannered as to follow a classmate into the toilet. It was after this, though, that things came to a head, quite literally. The whole sorry business started when a parent called to say that her daughters had "things" in their hair and pointed out that "they avoid one or two children for that reason".

Wisely, you might think, Miss Johnson sent out a letter to each mother warning them of "dangers to hair". This, of course, merely served to open the floodgates, with parents writing in to say that their daughters had been "troubled" before or to hint darkly that they had heard the problem mentioned in relation to other girls. Personal accusations really started to fly, however, when one mother actually named the girl she blamed for infecting her daughters. Inevitably other mothers retaliated in kind and the Headmistress herself was then accused of pointing the finger of blame at specific parents.

As if "things" in pupils' hair were not bad enough, the number of special pleas on the grounds of rather fragile constitutions had also started to grow, a factor which would lead to quite an outburst from Miss Johnson some twelve months later! The conviction among some parents that their children were quite delicate led to requests for them to rest after dinner, or to avoid running about, or to be allowed to arrive late because of difficulties with digestion. Two sisters' faddy eating habits—they tended to "live on nothing" and refused to eat potatoes or fat—had to be catered for, while the delicate appetite of another was not being helped by having to "scramble" for school dinners and not always managing to eat anything. This particular plight prompted the request that she should be urged to drink milk during the morning.

Two other children were being kept away for a term: one because of her health, another because "school excites her so". Assuming that this was not simply an excess of scholarly enthusiasm, she joined a number of girls who were less than ecstatic about going to school. One girl was simply very nervous, another hated having to answer in class and a third had been caught out lying about her late arrival, claiming she had had a tooth out. When the reason for the lie was investigated it turned out that the girl in question had walked to school rather than catching the Farnworth train because the other girls were "cold" to her. Then there was the case of the child who was simply lazy, according to her cousin, and could not be persuaded to get up in time either for breakfast or for school. A few days later her father, who had no intention of mollycoddling her, wrote to say that he hoped Miss Johnson would be strict with her over matters of punctuality. Furthermore, he said, if the school were to insist that his daughter stay for afternoon prep he certainly would not object.

Given the general background of ailments and sensitivities, real or imaginary—not to mention bad posture—it is not surprising that Miss Johnson was keen to establish a gymnasium at the school. As we have already seen she was very much her father's daughter in this, being a firm believer in the physical and mental benefits of vigorous exercise. Her initial requests to the governing body had eventually borne fruit in the December of 1891 when, having reported that several of the parents were also very enthusiastic about the idea, she was permitted to approach a Mr Madgwick with a view to setting up a class of Swedish exercises. Lest anyone should question the advisability of a man taking on this role in a girls' school, it would appear that his daughter was the one who eventually got the job.

Meanwhile there had been a number of staff changes: Miss Berry had been appointed as a replacement for Miss Horner who had left to pursue her studies in Oxford; Gertrude Sturges, who was by then an altogether happier pupil than during the affair of the torn book in 1888, had taken on the role of Student Teacher and in December Miss Edith Johnson had been appointed as Assistant Mistress. Born in South Africa, Edith was Miss Johnson's cousin, the daughter of her Uncle Henry Isaac who was Head of the Royal Institution School in Liverpool. So, with everything apparently sorted out satisfactorily, Miss Johnson must have felt reasonably optimistic about the annual Inspection which was scheduled for the following February.

Had she known beforehand, however, that the event would coincide with the furore about hair, she might not have been quite so sanguine! Nothing could be done about it, however, and in mid-February Mr Richard Booth duly arrived to inspect the school on behalf of the Cambridge University Local Examinations and Lectures Syndicate. Despite the atmosphere of nit-induced hostility and mistrust that was rife among the parents at the time, Mr Booth happily found nothing amiss. Indeed he praised the "admirable discipline and courtesy of the pupils". Not only that but he concluded that the "school is in my opinion progressing very favourably and … its condition is decidedly satisfactory."

One of the many reports sent to Dr William Horrocks GP and his wife, Mary, in the course of Mabel's school career.

We can only imagine the relief Miss Johnson must have felt when she read his comments on the hitherto benighted Geography teaching: "Forms V and IV had studied Asia and the British Possessions. The work of Form V was decidedly good. Mabel Horrocks obtained

77 per cent of the marks." Mabel must indeed have been blessed among pupils, especially in view of the following comments on English Grammar: "In Form V Mabel Horrocks again distinguished herself and in Form IV Annie Macbeth deserves special mention."

As had generally been the case—and perhaps surprisingly given the modern stereotype of girls finding Mathematics difficult—the comments about the subject were almost universally positive. "On the whole I consider the Mathematical work of the school to be decidedly encouraging," observed Mr Booth before going on to praise some of the younger girls for working accurately and intelligently on Euclid having studied the subject for just one term. Those older girls who sat Euclid papers were also praised for bringing their "thinking powers" into play with good results. However, he did note that in relation to Arithmetic a significant minority of the younger girls "would do well to pay more attention to the subject".

Meanwhile all the languages, ancient and modern, were judged to suffer from the same deficiency—"a slavish adherence to literalness of translation"—which was causing them to make mistakes. To counter this Mr Booth urged the pupils to aim for an idiomatic and spirited style. His final remarks related to the Kindergarten which he found "very interesting". He was particularly impressed by their Object lessons, implying that such a subject was not often provided at this level. Once again Miss Johnson's firm belief in the value of aesthetics and the early development of sensory intelligence was providing a very distinctive and forward-looking aspect to the curriculum.

Adding to the satisfaction Miss Johnson must have felt on another largely successful Inspection, was an increasing trend for both parents and pupils to set their sights firmly on examination success and the possibility of higher education. In September Mr Talbot had requested that his daughter Bessie be entered for the Oxford Senior examinations and by March Miss Johnson was writing to the parents of Mabel Horrocks, Lucy Wilding, Annie Macbeth, Katie Kenyon, Ethel Scrimgeour and Linda Haselden about the possibility of their trying for scholarships when they reached the age of fifteen. These particular scholarships were designed to encourage very able pupils to remain at the school for a further two or three years—and all of these girls were able with five of them having received special mention in Mr Booth's report.

Not all such enquiries were the occasion of unalloyed pleasure, however. Sometimes the "requests" were more like demands as was the case when one mother asked about scholarships and then added that she and her husband thought they had paid enough for their daughter's education and would like something in return! Miss Johnson's punctuation in the following entries also makes it clear that she thought some parental expectations were unrealistic: "Father anxious about her progress and that she should prepare for the College of Preceptors or Locals—with a view to going to College!" and "Father writes, wishing her to be pushed on in Euclid and Algebra, to begin a Latin author and to learn English Grammar! I propose an interview." Oh to have been a fly on the wall during that particular meeting!

A possible consequence of sights being set higher was the tendency of some girls to overwork in the pursuit of perfection, prompting yet more complaints about too many hours being spent on homework—to which Miss Johnson usually responded in a kindly, patient and sympathetic manner. Excessive hours being spent on homework could, of course, also be a sign that a child was struggling. This seems to be the case with a request for a pupil to be put down to a lower class because she was spending too long working in the evenings—her parents' additional complaint that she had been "neglected" in Scripture and had done hardly any History possibly indicating her lack of ability rather than any failing of the school. It also becomes clear that her parents had a real objection to Scripture because they wrote again demanding that she drop the subject on the grounds that the lessons were too "superstitious and worthless".

While the first Inspection in the new school had passed off very satisfactorily and a growing number of its pupils had clearly been inspired by Mrs Fawcett's exhortations to aim high, there were inevitably a few minor snags with regard to the new building itself. As early as November some mothers were complaining about the roughness of the playground and the passage to the children's entrance. Taps were also "imperfect" and the painting of the school was not yet complete, resulting in the governors deciding to withhold £20 from the Contractor until the job was done.

With the school having had to find £4031 for the land and the new building as well as £800 for regular expenditure that year—which, as well as the predictably heavy outgoings for salaries, gas, coal and water, also had to stretch to sundry items such as the purchase of "a crumb brush, tray and table cloth for the Mistresses' room and looking glasses for the lavatory"—it is not surprising that money was still owing to the bank. The governors, therefore, decided to send a circular to all shareholders in the company requesting loans at 4.5% interest. The loans, which could be for any amount from £20 to £700, would be repaid at such time as the funds of the Company permitted it. This was one of the first major decisions Mr William Haslam took after being appointed Chairman of the Governors on July 6th 1892.

The end of the academic year brought not only the prospect of the traditional summer gathering but also a sad event that must have affected Miss Johnson personally. Her cousin Edith had been obliged to leave in March because of her father's ill health. Sadly, Henry Johnson failed to rally and he died two months later at the age of sixty-four. Edith, feeling unable to return, resigned the following June and Miss Henley, who had been taken on as a temporary replacement, was asked to remain.

On an altogether happier note the pupils had a chance once again to demonstrate a variety of creative skills at the summer party held on June 23rd. Annoyingly, however, the weather meant that the planned outdoor events could not take place and both the presentation of the certificates by the Mayor, Mr William Nicholson, and the girls' performance of the cantata "The Village Queen" had to take place indoors. Another frustration, for us at least, is that there is no surviving record of what

Miss Johnson said in her annual report to parents—
which she had chosen to deliver at this same event
rather than at the end of the Autumn Term as she
normally did.

And so the academic year drew to a close, its final weeks
tinged with personal sadness for Miss Johnson at the loss
of her Uncle Henry and the departure from the school of
her cousin Edith.

Ap.13th Mother requests that she sh⁰
not sit in "draughts" She
has caught cold at school &
is "deaf" &c

Summer Term 1893
Ap.13th Complaint of lateness on
Friday —
Ap14th Aunt distressed at her report
& where does she learn to be
rough? She has come home
several times very late from
school [Edgar entered. has had his
eye turned - wears specs. in
strong light.
Ap.17th New child one of 6 — aged 15 —
very backward because of
irregular attendance — & has been
to Miss Coop's (?) St George's Rd.
has been ill, & helped mother with
domestic work — good at Drawing?
Ap.17th one of large family (5 at Miss
Coop's) very backward — has
dropped piano for 6 mons. fairly
strong —
Ap.20 I propose she should stay for
dinner & in afternoon for
curing laziness — Mother consents
turshes Oliver pushed on will. Drawi

April 1893.

113

Chapter 9

Treat this young thing tenderly

Despite the bad season, the Tennis Club had played many games over the summer of 1891 and had beaten arch-rivals Bury High School by 6 "setts" to 5—only to lose 4-1 in the return match two months later. Clara Berry's brother Arthur, who was a Fellow of King's College Cambridge, had delivered a lecture on "The Sun" illustrated with lantern slides and Maude Horner was thoroughly enjoying studying History at Lady Margaret Hall. She was particularly taken with Oxford's historic buildings, loved reading at the Radcliffe library and, of course, revelled in the student ritual of cocoa and chatter after an evening's work. She had even seen the great Mr Gladstone when he attended a service in the Cathedral: "a grand looking man" with a "very nice deep voice".

Yes, the greatest joy of 1893 is the treasure trove of information which suddenly opens up before us in the form of the first edition of the Bolton Girls' High School magazine. Craving indulgence on account of its extreme youth, the Editor begged the reader to "treat this young thing tenderly" and, tongue in cheek, justified its existence on the grounds of thorough egotism: "Our own children interest us more than anybody else's, our own chronicles are more important than those of the Great Mogul or of the Emperors of China, our own friends are nearer and dearer than the Man in the Moon." But the real reason for the new venture was to create a fresh link between past and present members of the school.

For those keen to get a fuller flavour of school life it could not be better. In its pages we discover the generosity of benefactors—parents, staff and former pupils alike—who donate pictures, museum specimens, butterfly collections, books and prizes. We learn about the Kyrle Society whose object was "to make the school look pretty" by purchasing pictures and other objects of interest and about Miss Berry's Design Society whose Lower Form members had been busily submitting designs for tiles, book covers, monograms, brooches and gates.

Here we find the Past and Present Club, whose numbers had doubled in a year, heavily involved in charitable work. Seven Old Girls had put on an entertainment for patients at the Blair Hospital, a convalescent home set up five years earlier in Bromley Cross. They also helped out at the local Girls' Club on Thursday nights, giving Object lessons, teaching "fancy work" and playing games. Badges were awarded to their young charges at the end of the year—presented by none other than Miss Johnson.

If it were not for the Magazine we would not know that Mr Coe, who had been so outraged by the singing of a non-Unitarian hymn at the opening of Park Road, seems not to have harboured a grudge for, just six months later, he had given a lecture on "Hamlet" to girls of the Upper School and twenty Old Girls. Nor would we know quite how many pictures adorned the walls of the new school, from Millet to Landseer, from Turner to Raphael, from portraits of great men and women in the Assembly Room to pictures of animals and children for the Third Form.

At the end of the Magazine there is a Calendar of Events for 1891 and 1892 and there we notice that, on October 17th 1892, Miss Johnson delivered a lecture on Tennyson. This was prompted not simply by her admiration of his work—nor indeed by her feeling somewhat proprietorial about him, having heard him reading "Maud" in her Uncle Alexander's drawing room when she was a girl—but also by the fact that he had died just eleven days earlier at the age of eighty-three.

The Magazine also dispenses advice. Miss Jarvis and Mabel Horrocks urge the girls to read more widely, begging them to disprove those who say that "the present generation do not care for and cannot read Dickens" and to read Mrs Gaskell "for she was of the North Country, and wrote in a delightful manner". They heartily recommend Tennyson and Milton, the historical novels of Scott and "works of travel" such as "Robinson Crusoe" and "Gulliver's Travels". A book, they say, is a faithful friend and counsellor "in all weathers" and "in all fortunes".

Three poems written by pupils offer a glimpse of the "harsh realities" of school life. While they are almost certainly tongue-in-cheek, it seems very open-minded of the Editor to print them. The first complains about having to exchange her toys for the "plague" of lessons and having to speak very quietly instead of being allowed to shriek. The second takes the line "Will you come into my parlour said the spider to the fly?" and turns the spider into the Headmistress, the parlour into her office and the fly into a child caught talking on the stairs. The third bemoans how often she has had a "lesson returned" and her name "taken down"—in other words added to the list of miscreants whose homework was substandard. She concludes that she might as well give up as, with such a bad record, she will never get to the top.

If her poem was intended to bring about a change in her teachers' hearts, it failed—as the minutes of a Staff Meeting held in October show. Discussing the system of "taking names down", the staff agreed that the punishment should be for "corrections undone, naughty talking, work not given in and shoes not changed and put away". For the pupil, the sting in the tail lay in the fact that reports were to "mention the number of weeks that the name has *not* been taken down". At least the information was to be presented to parents in a positive rather than a negative way, although it is doubtful whether any child saw it like that!

While the Magazine naturally presented the school's best face to the world, the Headmistress's log inevitably continued to highlight problems, from children "learning to be rough" at school to others being caught copying. As regards actual lessons, Algebra and Euclid phobias seem to crop up a lot, encouraged no doubt by the view of some parents that such subjects were "so unnecessary for girls" and a "waste of time". Then, rather recklessly in view of Miss Johnson's strong aesthetic leanings, one father wrote to say that he wanted his daughter to be a teacher and therefore did not wish her to learn such things as Arts and Crafts as they would not be beneficial. Outraged, Miss Johnson replied tersely that "Arts and Crafts are essential to a liberal education"—but he remained unconvinced.

Setting aside one seemingly very genuine plea for "special indulgence" — made by a mother who said that her daughter Grace was "not 'stupid or inattentive' but only very deaf and not at all well" — parental over-sensitivities on behalf of their children were becoming more noticeable. One father interpreted a set of report comments as being too reserved, saying that his daughter felt they were unfair and that people were prejudiced against her, while a Mrs Munro expressed a sense of "hurt" that no-one had enquired about her daughter's absence.

On one occasion we get a glimpse of differences of opinion at home when, unbeknown to his wife, a father wrote to "complain of stooping probably due to wrong-sized desk — also of 'slip-slop' Arithmetic teaching". By chance it was his wife who opened the reply from Miss Johnson. She was clearly mortified to discover the kind of accusations her husband had been levelling at the school behind her back and immediately sent in an apology.

Then there are the slightly puzzling entries such as the one which notified the school that a child was "to go finally abroad and get rid of prejudices" and another about a girl leaving because she was "half-engaged". Most importantly, however, this was the year in which attendance exercised Miss Johnson's mind more than ever before. As had become clear in the previous academic year, she was beginning to lose patience with parents who treated their children like delicate specimens or kept them away for no very good reason. Hence the following forthright remark to parents at the end of the academic year: "I once heard of a schoolmaster who said that every mother cherished two ideas about her boy: one, that he was very clever and, two, that he was very delicate. A certain number of girls appear to be very delicate and their delicacy is rather apt to lie in the direction of Euclid and Algebra."

She was driven to spell out the consequences of unnecessary absences: lagging behind, slowing the rest of the class down while the child in question was being "dragged up painfully to the point which the others have reached", or even losing the desire to work completely. What had particularly annoyed her was the fact that, on the morning after a fortnight's Whit holiday in 1893, thirty-three children out of the total of ninety had failed to appear—"although the long holiday of the year was known to be approaching," she added in exasperation. Most frustratingly, this was despite her determined efforts to be accommodating—at the beginning of the year she had invited all sixty-three mothers to attend a meeting to discuss holiday dates. Only sixteen had bothered to attend!

Suddenly we find her urging what sounds very much like a home-school contract. Bemoaning the growing tendency "to allow obstacles to be inevitable which in older and severer days would have been set aside" she suggested that there ought to be "an implied contract that the engagement which binds a teacher to meet her pupils at certain times, days and hours is equally binding on the child."

Despite the clear affection of her parents, Miss Johnson's own upbringing had been quite stern—hence her remark about "older and severer days". From the start William and Harriet Johnson had impressed upon their children that "one of the chief virtues of a child was obedience to its elders, parents and teachers, and that discipline played a large part in its education". As an adult Miss Johnson's reaction to this seems to have been that, while fully endorsing firm discipline, she preferred to exercise it in a more spontaneous and flexible way. Hence her distress when the growing laxness of some parents seemed to be giving her little option but to adopt a system that was altogether more "formal and forced" than she would have liked.

Citing a pimply face as a reason for absence might or might not have been a cause for annoyance, but it was more than just absences that had triggered her "rant" about feeble-mindedness and mollycoddling. Numerous children it seems were subject to fits of crying or were not to be pressed for fear of them breaking down "at any moment". One child had to be allowed to take tonic wine, another was not to eat sweets or pastry and another was to leave off gymnastics because of a bad back and twitching eye. Tiredness was given as a reason for dropping Drill and another child was not to hurry from the train as she had "been suffering much with head". A complaint about one pupil having allegedly caught cold because she was required to change her shoes provoked the snappy retort, "I suggest galoshes". To add to it all, while many parents had always chosen to keep the school informed about whether their daughter's "change"—that is, her period—had or had not begun, many such comments now started to reveal a tendency to regard menstruation as an ailment rather than part of a natural cycle. Indeed, one child was withdrawn for half a term because her periods were irregular.

Not everyone was the same, however. Some parents believed in a certain level of stoicism—just like Miss Johnson's own mother and father. One girl was returning after a serious illness which had affected her heart; the Briscoe parents, who had lost three children to scarlet fever some years earlier, wrote to say that despite the doctor advising their daughter to stay away from school altogether they thought her "better to be doing something, so she is to come for the morning and do *no* home lessons"; and a Mrs Bradshaw did not "care for Annie to lie down after dinner, as I proposed, but would rather she prepared lessons on wet days and played on fine days". Annie survived the lack of an afternoon sleep and later went on to study at the University of Liverpool.

Miss Johnson's conclusion seems to have been that some at least of the numerous ailments and difficulties owed more to a child being work-shy and spoilt than to anything else. Her remedy was, therefore, a no-nonsense one. She urged regular attendance at afternoon preparation arguing that, as children began to cope with their work better, they might find it more pleasurable and, consequently, headaches would grow "surprisingly few and far between". Clearly a firm believer in the influence of the mind over the body, she said that "a mind braced to physical effort conquers fatigue and by that very fact the body is strengthened rather than weakened."

Exhortations to parents to be rather firmer and less indulgent did not always bear fruit, however. Within days of Miss Johnson's "rant", a mother had allowed her children to stay off for the Royal Wedding of the Duke of York to Princess Victoria of Teck on July 6th 1893. "I remonstrate" was the world-weary comment added at the end of the entry. Maybe dealing with such irritations was beginning to take its toll on her.

There were pressures elsewhere, too. By October Miss Berry had been ordered to rest and Miss Bowes had been appointed on a temporary basis. Rather happily for Miss Johnson, Miss Bowes was in fact none other than her young cousin Janet, the twenty-two year old daughter of her Aunt Fanny and Uncle Robert. Drafting in cousins to help out was becoming something of a habit! Miss Berry's health did not improve, however, and by February the following year the governors had, with much regret, accepted her resignation. On the brighter side, however, a Miss Livingstone was engaged as a Mathematical Mistress—this departure from the normal job description possibly signalling a move towards greater staff specialisation.

In terms of pupil numbers recruitment was going quite well. Pleasingly, half the entries during the academic year were for the Kindergarten, showing, Miss Johnson felt, an increased confidence in the management of the lower part of the school. Perhaps word was also getting out that the younger children were doing exciting things like clay modelling, river walks and pond dipping! The chance to train children from the very beginning of their school life mattered a great deal to Miss Johnson, as did the retention of able girls through to the highest forms. Her plea for girls to be encouraged to stay on also shows that the stereotypical Year 9 switch-off is nothing new:

The Whole School, Whitsuntide 1892.

"Every teacher knows that the best working years for a healthy child are from eight to twelve, then again from fifteen to eighteen approximately and therefore a backward child of thirteen who only stays with us for a year or two cannot be expected to do us or herself much credit."

As regards the nine girls who were then in the Sixth and Fifth Form, Miss Johnson spoke highly of their industry and loyalty to good school traditions, adding that "nothing of course affects the whole tone of a school so well as a good standard of ability and character among the elder girls." Amongst the older girls' successes were those of Bessie Talbot who had been awarded a Leaving Scholarship—having secured a place at Owen's College to study Natural Sciences—and of Mabel Horrocks and Katie Kenyon who, on the basis of their very good performances in the July examinations, had been awarded Continuation Scholarships for their remaining time at school.

Meanwhile those things that are pleasing to the senses, in whatever form, continued to count a great deal. Mrs Haslam and Miss Curtis were asked to arrange for the walls of the classrooms to be thoroughly cleaned and "beautified" and Mrs Haslam was also instructed to purchase a rug and cushion for the couch in the Mistresses' room. On a somewhat loftier plane, Miss Johnson had spotted a second-hand grand piano—a Broadwood no less—being offered for sale for £50 and was given permission to buy it for the school. There had also been a gratifying increase in numbers taking music—fourteen for piano and five for violin. Excellent teachers had been recruited and Miss Johnson's stated aim that music should become a more serious study, with pupils being prepared for Higher Musical Examinations, moved a step closer. Her grandfather would not have approved!

Given the earlier attack by one father on the value of Arts and Crafts, it is no surprise to find Miss Johnson very publicly and pointedly defending them. "An alternation from headwork to handwork is perhaps one of the most distinctive principles and the most universally held by modern educators," she said. She remained utterly committed to fostering both the "taste for beauty and the faculty of producing it" — the work of creation being, she argued, "the highest of all pleasures". For this reason she was proud of the fact that, as far as she knew, her pupils were offered a wider range of crafts than was available at most other schools. As befitted these sentiments, June brought with it an Arts and Crafts Exhibition at which a variety of work done by the pupils was on display. The attendance was very good and the visitors thoroughly enjoyed the occasion which included performances by the school choirs and band as well as a "converzasione" at 5.30 pm.

Unusually, there was no gradual winding down to the end of term in 1893 for the Inspection that academic year did not take place until July. This change was as a result of Miss Johnson's decision the previous October that the examinations of the school should in future be conducted by the "Oxford and Cambridge Examinations Board" instead of the "Cambridge Syndicate". As she had explained to parents, the new exams were not only of a higher quality but, more importantly, they were "more elastic" in their arrangements, allowing the school greater freedom to judge for itself the age at which a candidate should be entered for a particular level of paper. This was bound to appeal to a Headmistress for whom the needs of individual pupils would, wherever possible, always take precedence over rigid systems.

In his report to the Board, Mr A Wilkins MA of St John's College Cambridge, began by praising the excellent order and discipline, the brightness and cheerfulness of the pupils and, most gratifyingly, the "unusually attractive" building. He also concluded that the teaching had evidently been "bright, interesting and on the best lines". Yet, his comments in relation to the oral part of the examination for the Upper School, were disappointing: "the standard did not appear to be high," he said, "and there were few girls of special promise" — although he did concede that this might have been because most of their best work had been reserved for testing by written examination.

There were a number of low points in fact. The oral examination of Form II had suggested that "there were several backwards girls in this class" while many of Form IV's written answers on Arithmetic were so far below standard that "no meaning could be attached" to them. Papers on Scripture Knowledge revealed that "a great part of the work requires improvement" while the English compositions demonstrated "little knowledge of the primary rules of order and arrangement".

The day was saved, however, by the continuing success of the Object lessons for the five little girls and four little boys of the Kindergarten and by the good progress being made in French not only in Form I who were being taught "by a method not commonly in use" — frustratingly no indication of the method was given — but throughout the school, particularly in translation. Amongst the older girls some familiar names had also saved the day by producing some excellent papers on English History which had prompted quite fulsome praise. Those singled out for special commendation were: Mabel Horrocks, Katie Kenyon, Annie Bradshaw and Beatrice Jameson. At least two of these girls would go on to university: Katie to Newnham and, as we have already seen, Annie to University College, Liverpool.

With ninety-two pupils on roll the school was edging closer to the longed-for target of one hundred. It was also about to appoint two new teachers, Miss Marion Rowland for the Kindergarten and Miss Shorrock to teach Chemistry — the latter being destined to add to the school's already quite impressive Oxbridge "presence" when, after a year or so, she left to study at Somerville.

And so the school year ended and the long holiday beckoned. Scarcely anyone, we assume, could have had an inkling of what the Autumn Term would bring.

June. . Notice : leaving Bolton –

June. Correspondence as to whether she should have lunch Mother says "yes" tho' child continually says she does not wish it –

June 24th. To be kept at home till end of term for health – & Mabel to leave off French.

June 30th. Mrs M. writes that she has caught cold – from an open window.

July 6th. Mother gives them holiday for Royal Wedding I remonstrate.

July 21st. Mother gives fortnight's notice I remonstrate – She calls to explain –

July 24th. Mother calls to explain absence on account of pimply face!

July 25. Notice – to have a governess on account of health –

July . To be withdrawn from exam˜ on acct of health – & the fees to be returned if possible –

July . Mother calls to consult about future. & I suggest private governess –

Miss Johnson's final log entries, June–July 1893.

128

Chapter 10

Rest, change and new horizons

"Owing to Miss Johnson being ill at the opening of the School, Miss Jarvis has been obliged to take the temporary management."

This short statement is the first indication we have of there being anything amiss. Alarm was probably not too widespread at that point because Miss Johnson was still very much involved in decision making, as we can see from the fact that Fannie Jarvis contacted her for advice about a parent who objected to his daughter not being put up into a higher form. As the girl had missed a whole term Miss Jarvis felt she would be far better staying put, a view which Miss Johnson firmly endorsed from her sick bed saying that the girl "must stay where she is". By early October, however, there had been no improvement in Miss Johnson's health and it was thought "advisable for her to take the remainder of the term for rest and change". Consequently, an additional teacher, Miss Chapman, was engaged to assist Miss Jarvis.

Just a month later, the governors' worst fears were confirmed. A letter was received from Miss Johnson, announcing that she would be standing down owing to her continuing poor health. With little option to do otherwise, the governing body accepted her resignation which was to take effect at the end of the Autumn Term. "At the same time," the minutes continued, "much sympathy was expressed for Miss Johnson and regret that she should feel obliged to resign. The Secretary was instructed to write to Miss Johnson to this effect."

She had achieved so much in five short years— establishing a Kindergarten and a thoroughgoing commitment to the Arts and Crafts, overseeing the move to purpose-built premises, almost doubling the pupil population, increasing the take-up of external examinations, encouraging and enabling a significant number of girls to go on to university,[12] not to mention setting up an Old Girls' Association and launching the School Magazine. Now that she would no longer be in charge it must have seemed as though a brilliant light had suddenly been extinguished.

With little time to spare, an advertisement for a Headmistress was inserted in the "Atheneum" with the instruction that applications should be sent in before November 23rd. The decision was also taken to raise the Headmistress's salary to £250. Appointment procedures seem to have been far less protracted in those days: on the closing day for applications the governors duly selected three candidates—Miss Clarke, Miss Dymond and Miss Freeman—for interview the following Thursday at 3.00 pm. By the end of that afternoon it had been unanimously decided to appoint Miss Dymond. In

---

[12] In addition to the college and university places mentioned elsewhere in the text we know that Winifred Matthews went to Newnham in 1895 to study Medieval and Modern Languages [she later taught in France and various schools in England before becoming Headmistress of Dulwich High School in 1909] and that Annie Macbeth went on to Glasgow School of Art. There will almost certainly have been other pupils from Miss Johnson's time who went on to Higher Education whose names and details are unfortunately not known to us.

the words of young William Haslam, who would have been about five when he first encountered her, she was "a formidable person, with olive complexion, large hands, dressed always with a flowing jacket, a waistcoat and long skirts".

Her credentials were impressive. Born in Worcester in 1862 and educated at Cheltenham College, she had gone up to Newnham to study Mathematics in 1882—the same year in which she was awarded a BA from London University. Having successfully passed her Mathematics Tripos in 1885 she had worked as an Assistant Mistress at Shrewsbury High School from 1886-1887 and then at Bedford High School from 1887-1888. A brief career change then followed in which she worked for a year as Assistant Librarian at the People's Palace in Mile End—a ground-breaking educational and cultural centre for the local community, the library of which was modelled on that of the British Museum. Then, from 1891-1893, she had taught at the Perse Girls' School in Cambridge.

This was to be a very successful appointment with Miss Dymond remaining at the school until 1919. She was a tireless worker whom the 1906 Inspection hailed as "very capable", applauding her good influence on the girlhood of Bolton. She introduced a school uniform and compulsory games but the most significant event in her time as Headmistress was the amalgamation in 1913 of Bolton Grammar School for Boys and the High School for Girls—the new Foundation formally coming into existence on April 1 1915.

The Joint Foundation which was to be known as Bolton School, as it still is today, was endowed by the first

Viscount Leverhulme, then Sir William Hesketh Lever. His aim was to build "an abode of good learning" which by its architectural beauty and perfection of detail would influence its members during their school lives and afterwards, enabling them to become "good citizens and true servants of their generation". However, the outbreak of the First World War meant that it was not until 1919, the year in which Miss Meade took over as Headmistress from Miss Dymond, that C T Adshead's stunning design for a school of 400 boys and 400 girls was finally accepted—and even Miss Meade had to wait until 1928 for construction to get fully under way.

But what of Fanny Eliza Johnson in the meantime? Well, the first news of her after her resignation comes from the School Magazine of 1894 which announces that "we have the most cheering reports of her from Italy, where she is travelling". Her choice of recuperative venue is not surprising as, at the end of her first Summer Term as Headmistress, she had given a lecture on Italian painting and in 1893 had donated copies of a Giotto fresco and Botticelli's "Madonna and Child" to the school. Then, in the autumn of 1894, fully recovered, she returned to Bolton to give a lecture to the Old Girls on her travels, complete with lantern slides, photographs and sketches. Nor was this to be her last visit to the school for we know that, at the very least, she attended an Old Girls' Reunion in November 1909 to which past members of staff had been invited—much to the delight of her former pupils.

Following her successful lecture on her travels round Italy, the next time we find her is in the 1901 census aged forty-five. At that point she was living in Chelsea with her younger brothers Reginald Brimley and Augustine. It is not really a surprise to discover that, while Reginald was a writer[13] and publisher and Augustine a publisher's clerk, Fanny Eliza was busily pursuing her own career as an author. Then, at some point after the sale of Llandaff House in 1902, she went back to Cambridge and, along with William Ernest and Alice, moved to Newnham, to a house on Millington Road near to their sister Harriet's school. Appropriately named Ramsey House in memory of their grandfather William's birthplace, it was evidently here that Fanny Eliza did most of her writing.[14]

She seems to have had a particular interest in German literature and in 1922 produced what may well have been her most significant work: "The German mind as reflected in their literature from 1870 to 1914". However, the majority of her books arose out of her love of amateur dramatics coupled with her awareness of the desperate need for good play scripts for use in schools. She began in 1907, adapting dramatic scenes from history and from English Literature and ended in the 1920s with "The Little Duke and other historical plays" and "Earth and her Children"—a pageant play which was published by her Uncle Robert's company, Bowes and Bowes. In addition to all her writing, Fanny Eliza

---

[13] A great supporter of the fight for women's equality and access to the same education as men, Reginald devoted much of his critical attention to women authors and literary figures such as Mrs Thrale—a close friend of Fanny Burney and Dr Johnson—who held celebrated literary salons and was herself extremely sympathetic to "women of literature and erudition".

[14] While we cannot be absolutely sure, it appears very likely that "Fanny Johnson", the author of the works cited here, is indeed our Fanny Johnson.

had also shouldered the extra responsibility of looking after her nephews, seven-year-old Charles and four-year-old Stephen, after the untimely death of her brother William's wife Barbara in 1904.

Ramsey House saw numerous visitors over the years and it was there, between 1908 and 1911, that she entertained William Haslam—by then a History student at King's College. This was the selfsame William who had escaped humiliation by having his "Little Lord Fauntleroy" locks shorn before entering the Kindergarten and who many years later would teasingly describe himself as one of the oldest "Old Girls" of Bolton High School for Girls. He had applied to King's not only because of its distinguished academic record but also because Fanny Johnson and Clara Berry, who had been such close friends of the Haslam family when they taught in Bolton, both had brothers who were Fellows of King's in 1908.

Recalling his visits to Ramsey House, William noted that Fanny—whom he described as being "quite a feature" during his time at Cambridge—had been full of "well-meaning amateurish magicals" and very intense. "One had to be careful," he added somewhat cryptically, "not to be caught in her traps." It was probably there, too, when she was quite an old woman in the mid-1930s that Fanny had her portrait painted by Delmar Banner and, possibly at the same time, a sketch of herself done by his wife, the noted sculptor Josefina de Vasconcellos.

Ramsey House remained Fanny's home for over forty years—far longer than she had spent at Llandaff House which was eventually demolished in 1932. On February

7th 1943, she died of cardiac failure brought on by gastric influenza. She was eighty-seven. William Ernest and Alice had both died a number of years earlier and so it fell to her nephew Charles William Heaton Johnson, who had been with her when she died, to notify the Registrar.

Fanny Eliza Johnson in old age.
Painted in the 1930s by the noted sculptor Josefina de Vasconcellos
(Mrs Delmar Banner).

The funeral took place four days later on Thursday February 11th at St Marks' Church—only a matter of yards from her home. Charles Johnson was there, of course, and her brother George's daughters, Gladys and Madge, along with members of the Bowes family and, representing the Macmillans, her second cousin Rachael Dyer.[15] Among the non-family mourners were her domestic staff — Miss Watwood, Mrs Suggitt and Mr Barton — as well as a number of academics and figures from the world of politics. These included the Provost of King's College, Professors Broad, Robertson and Wilson, Lady Katherine Oldfield, suffragist Mrs Vulliamy who was also a neighbour and old friend of the family, three representatives from the Cambridge Labour Party and Mrs Wishart of the Women's International League. Also present was Dr Anna Keilin who had certified Fanny Eliza's death and had possibly attended her in her final hours. Following the service she was cremated and her ashes strewn in the Garden of Remembrance at Cambridge City Crematorium.

Meanwhile, of course, life had been carrying on for a number of her former colleagues at the High School. In February 1894, a few weeks after Miss Dymond's arrival, Fannie Jarvis had been granted a month's extension of her Easter holiday in recognition of the fact that her health had suffered from the extra burdens imposed by Miss Johnson's absence. It is possible that she was still not back to full strength by the following autumn. Whatever the reason, she finally resigned on October 3rd 1894.

---

[15] Rachael was the granddaughter of Fanny's Aunt Caroline and Uncle Alexander. In 1889 her mother, Margaret Anne Macmillan, had married Chicago-born Louis Dyer, writer and graduate of Balliol College, Oxford. In the late 1890s he became a lecturer in Modern Languages at Balliol.

However, by 1901 all was well again and she appeared in the census of that year as the Head of a private school in Folkestone, the beguiling address of which was "Conamura", Audley Cottage, The Riviera, Sandgate. Among her five staff members we find not only her own sister Nellie but also Clara Berry who is described as her partner in the business. It is fascinating to see that, among the thirteen boarders, were three girls from Bolton: Josephine Haselden, Millicent Dutton and Mildred Knowles. Two of these at least—Josephine and Mildred—were from the High School. Whether their presence in Folkestone was as a result of devotion to Miss Jarvis or a desperate search for healthy sea air we cannot tell.

Meanwhile, after completing her History degree at Lady Margaret Hall, former teacher Maude Horner had gone on to become Headmistress of Sale High School. In 1904 she married Francis Holland and later worked at Kendal High School.

Kate Vokins—who had preceded Fanny Johnson as Headmistress and had then gone on to the headship of Blackburne House School in Liverpool—had emigrated to India in 1891 to take up the post of Principal of the Maharani's school in Mysore where she started a class for child widows. It has been suggested that these children may have been ostracised as a result of having failed to commit suttee, the practice whereby widows were expected to burn themselves to death on their husband's funeral pyres. Kate worked there until 1897, dying in Bombay on June 4th at the very early age of forty-six.

As far as our most frequently cited students are concerned, their lives had moved on apace. Laura Brackenbury, who had gone up to Newnham in 1890, had not only gained the Cobden Scholarship for distinguished success in Political Economics in 1892 but had gone on to gain 1st Class in the Moral Sciences Tripos—Psychology, Logic and Economics—in 1893. She then worked in several training colleges before becoming the Principal of Graystoke Place Training College from 1907 to 1933, with a five-year break from 1915 when she served as an Inspector of Schools for London County Council.

She wrote "A Primer of Psychology" and "The Teaching of Grammar", which stressed the link between Logic and Grammar, as well as a book intriguingly entitled "The Teaching of Housewifery in Belgium". Increasingly deaf herself, she did a great deal to promote educational opportunities for teachers who dealt with children who had disabilities. Towards the end of her life she returned to her birthplace, the Isle of Wight, dying there on May 12th 1937 aged sixty-nine.

Katie Kenyon who became Head Girl in Miss Dymond's time had gone up to Newnham to study Classics in 1896. Her first teaching post was as an Assistant Mistress at Penrhos College, Colwyn Bay. One year later she moved on to Ellerslie School in Manchester before setting up her own private school in 1902. In 1906 she married Percy Sidlow Crowther and they had two daughters. Returning to her Farnworth roots she became a governor of Farnworth Grammar School and the first Honorary Secretary of the Farnworth Women's Suffrage Society. She died on February 26th 1967.

Headmistress Miss Dymond and Senior Girls, 1895.

[Back row] Daisy Frankland, Elsie Atherton, Ethel Scrimgeour, Trixie Jameson.

[Front row] Winifred Matthews, Miss Dymond, Mabel Horrocks, Fanny Smethurst, Katie Kenyon.

Ethel Scrimgeour and Fanny Smethurst had also gone up to Newnham in 1896 to read Mathematics. Ethel spent two years there and left without taking her Tripos examination, choosing instead to return to the High School as a teacher. She stayed there until 1903 when she married Dr William Bateman JP. They had three sons and one daughter and in later years she became an Infant Welfare Worker and served as Chairman of the Rochdale Welfare Mission. She died on August 6th 1960.

Having passed her Mathematics Tripos in 1899 Fanny Smethurst went on to enjoy a long career in education. After teaching at Richmond Girls' School she spent four years at Bath High School, followed by one year as a

Junior Lecturer at Clapham Day Training College. Her final posts were at St Pancras County Secondary School where she stayed for five years followed by an impressive twenty-five years at Plumstead County Secondary School. She retired at sixty but lived for another thirty-six years, dying on October 21st 1974.

In 1892, aged fifteen, Winifred Haslam had gone to board at Wimbledon High School. Throwing herself into her new life with great enthusiasm she served on the committees of the Art, Tennis and Hockey Clubs. Then, in 1894, at the age of eighteen, she left school for good. It is not absolutely clear when she returned to Bolton but certainly by the mid-1890s she had re-established links with the High School and was acting as the Honorary Secretary for the Old Girls' Association. In 1902 she married Oliver Winder, an engineer whose father was the notable Boltonian Thomas Henry Winder, solicitor and clerk to the justices. Eventually she and her husband moved to Sheffield.

In the years following Fanny Eliza's resignation as Headmistress, life had continued to be very eventful and productive for her siblings, their centre of operations continuing to be mainly in Cambridge.

In 1893 her father had finally retired at the age of sixty-seven at which point her sister Harriet—together with her young cousin Janet Bowes who had just returned from her brief stint at Bolton High School for Girls—decided to turn Llandaff House academy into a mixed preparatory school for younger children. When the house was sold in 1902—the same year as her late marriage to the brilliant mathematician, Arthur

Berry[16]—Harriet initially moved her school to Grange Road before acquiring newly-built premises five years later. She remained in charge until her retirement in 1925 at the age of seventy, a year after her husband had become Vice Provost of King's. Harriet and Arthur both died in 1929.

One of the reasons for the sale of Llandaff House in 1902 was that William Henry Farthing Johnson, the man who had done so much to mould his children's opinions, values and beliefs, had died on July 16th 1901. He was seventy-six. The obituary which appeared in the local newspaper described him as one of the most formative influences on the early lives of many notable men in Cambridgeshire. Fittingly, William Johnson's coffin was carried to the chapel along a route that took it down the garden of Llandaff House and then on through his beloved Grove—a place for which he had always had an "almost religious devotion".

We do not know whether his eldest daughter Lucy was able to attend the funeral as, according to the census of that year, it seems that she was working as an elocution teacher in Margate. While we cannot be absolutely certain that this was indeed the same Lucy, it does seem quite likely as other teaching roles would have been very

---

[16] He was none other than the brother of Clara Berry who had delivered a lecture on the Sun at the High School and who, along with William Johnson, had been partly responsible for William Haslam applying to King's. During WW1 he had encoded Kitchener's despatches concerning the evacuation of Gallipoli and had worked for the Naval Air Service in Egypt. He was awarded an OBE.

difficult for her, if not impossible, given the fact that she must have been virtually blind by then.

Fanny Eliza's youngest sister Alice continued in her role as Secretary to Mrs Eleanor Sidgwick, the Principal of Newnham College, until 1903. Indeed, she may well have been the one who suggested the idea of Mrs Sidgwick going up to Bolton to address the school in 1896. For many years Alice was also a member of the Society for Psychical Research taking on the roles of secretary, research officer and editor of the society's journal. Along with such luminaries as Professor and Mrs Sidgwick, she worked for four years on the society's Census of Hallucinations and also devoted considerable time to the study of automatic writing.[17] A "loyal daughter of Newnham" and a lifelong supporter of women's rights, Alice died on January 13th 1940.

William Ernest Johnson, the mathematician and logician, had married Barbara Keymer Heaton, the daughter of a lecturer in Chemistry at Charing Cross Hospital, in 1895. In 1902 he obtained a Fellowship at King's and taught there as Sidgwick lecturer in Moral Science. He went on to earn considerable fame as a result of his three volume work "Logic" — not to mention a fellowship of the British Academy and a number of honorary degrees. He also taught Mathematical Economics, one of his students being John Maynard Keynes who would become one of the twentieth century's most influential economists. Interestingly, Maynard Keynes had received his early education at Llandaff House at the hands of Harriet.

---

[17] She also collaborated with Richard Hodgson on Frederic Myers' major work "Human Personality" following the author's death before its completion.

Remarkably, William Johnson continued to lecture into his early seventies. He died on January 14th 1931 at the age of seventy-two having been admitted to St Andrew's Psychiatric Hospital, Northampton—which by a strange and poignant twist of fate was the same institution in which his mother had died four decades earlier.

George William Johnson, who worked for the Colonial Office, was also a committed champion of the suffragists, attending many of their meetings and never losing an opportunity to promote the cause. He joined in the first great suffragist procession through the streets of London and provided tireless administrative help during the election campaign of one of the first female candidates for Parliament, Mrs Oliver Strachey. But the support which required the most moral courage was that which he and his wife Lucy Nutter offered unstintingly to Josephine E Butler—the feminist who campaigned doggedly and at considerable personal cost against the "white slave trade" of prostitution. Despite this being a deeply unpopular cause—and a taboo topic in all polite circles—George and Lucy risked public censure by writing a memoir of Josephine Butler which came to be regarded as one of the most important contributions to her work. George died on February 13th 1926.

So, Fanny Eliza had outlived all of her siblings. As they had been so involved in the struggle for women's emancipation, their reaction to her death certificate would have been interesting. Under the column for occupation it simply states: "Spinster. Daughter of William Henry Farthing Johnson, a private schoolmaster, deceased." It is amazing to think that, as recently as 1943, a woman's "occupation" was usually only recorded in terms of her relationship to a man. No matter how much Fanny Eliza had loved and admired her father, this seems small return for her twenty years in education and her subsequent career as an author. There was still a long way to go before women were the equal of men in the eyes of the law.

Portrait of Fanny Eliza Johnson believed to have been painted by Delmar Banner in the 1930s.

Acknowledgments

While the bulk of the material for this book comes from the archives of Bolton School Girls' Division, a number of other sources have provided information for which the author is greatly indebted. These mainly relate to the Unitarian involvement with Bolton Girls' High School (1), the history of the Johnson family and Llandaff House Academy (2 & 3), and the shared experiences of girls' day schools in the nineteenth century (4).

Sources consulted

1. G M Ramsden: *A Responsible Society. The Life and Times of the Congregation of Bank Street Chapel, Bolton, Lancashire.* G Ramsden. 1985.

2. Alice Johnson: *George William Johnson: Civil Servant and Social Worker.* Printed for Private Circulation, Cambridge. 1927.

3. Kenneth Parsons: "Nonconformist School; the story of Llandaff House and its academy." *Cambridgeshire Local History Council Bulletin*, no. 39 pp. 1-8. 1984.

4. Gillian Avery: *The Best Type of Girl, A History of Girls' Independent Schools.* Andre Deutsch. 1991.

C Crowther, "Women on Sufferance", article on pp 37-39 of *A Newnham Anthology* ed. Ann Phillips, London, Cambridge University Press. 1979.

English Baptist Records, Volume 2. Church Book: St Andrew's Street Baptist Church, Cambridge 1720-1832 ed. Roger Hayden. Baptist Historical Society. 1991

Margaret Higginson: Appendix to *The History of Bolton School.* W E Brown, MA. Bolton School. 1976.

William Johnson: *Thoughts on Education: an Address delivered to the Friends and Supporters of the Llandaff-House Academy, Regent Street.* London. 1830.

J J O'Connor and E F Robertson: *William Ernest Johnson,* an article at www.history.mcs.st-andrews.ac.uk February 2005.

John Archibald Venn: *Alumni Cantabrigiensis, Part 2, 1752-1900.*

www.ancestry.co.uk
www.newn.cam.ac.uk/archive
www.spartacus.schoolnet.co.uk

We are also indebted to the following people for their generous help in tracking down details of the lives not only of the Johnsons but also of pupils and staff of the school:

Patricia Ackerman and Anne Thomson: Newnham College Archives, Cambridge
Clare Button: Archives Assistant, Oxford University Archives, Bodleian Library
Gillian Cooke: Group Archivist, Cambridge Assessments
Elizabeth Ennion: Assistant Archivist, King's College, Cambridge
Maya Evans: Development Assistant, Lady Margaret Hall, Oxford
Anna Flood: Archives Assistant, Royal Holloway, University of London
Katy Iliffe: Librarian, Sedbergh School
Chris Jakes: Cambridge Local Studies Library
Kelly Jones: Librarian, Wimbledon High School
Kathryn Lynn: Bolton News Library

Katie Mooney: Assistant Archivist, Institute of Education, University of London
Sue Neville and Gill Shapland: Archivists, County Record Office, Cambridge
Kate Perry: Archivist, Girton College, Cambridge
Christina Raven Conn: Librarian, Nottingham Local Studies Library
Alexa Rees: Archivist, Nottinghamshire Archives
Alysoun Sanders: Archivist, Macmillan publishers
Barbara Selin: Administrative Officer, Bereavement Services, Cambridge City Crematorium
Anthony J Simpson: Cambridge Family History Society member
Sue Slack: Milton Road Library, Cambridge
Dr Gill Sutherland: Historian, Newnham College, Cambridge
Don Wenham: Chairman, Cambridge Family History Society

We should like to thank Fahad Mohamed, Bolton Girls' School Division ICT Support Assistant, for his great help with the illustrations.

Finally, but by no means least, we should like to thank Margaret Dickinson, Robert Millington, Gill Richards, Pamela Taylor and Jane Whitehead for reading the manuscript and for their very generous and helpful comments.

Printed in the United Kingdom
by Lightning Source UK Ltd.
131338UK00001B/70-453/P